ADMINISTRATIVE LAW

SECOND EDITION

By

RICHARD J. PIERCE, JR.
Lyle T. Alverson Professor of Law
George Washington University

CONCEPTS AND INSIGHTS SERIES®

FOUNDATION PRESS
2012

THOMSON REUTERS™

© 2008 FOUNDATION PRESS
© 2012 By THOMSON REUTERS/FOUNDATION PRESS

> 1 New York Plaza, 34th Floor
>
> New York, NY 10004
>
> Phone Toll Free 1–877–888–1330
>
> Fax 646–424–5201
>
> foundation–press.com

Printed in the United States of America

ISBN 978–1–60930–113–2

Mat #41240066

PREFACE

This book is written primarily to help law students understand the basics of federal administrative law. It emphasizes the powers of agencies, the ways in which they exercise those powers, the procedures they use to take actions of various types, and the relationships between agencies and the three branches of government-executive, legislative, and judicial. It does not discuss state or local administrative law. The legal systems and doctrines applicable to state and local agencies are too vast and variable to be susceptible to a treatment that is both accurate and concise.

RICHARD J. PIERCE, JR.

TABLE OF CONTENTS

ADMINISTRATIVE LAW

Chapter One

INTRODUCTORY OVERVIEW

Administrative law is the study of the roles of government agencies in the U.S. legal system, including the relationships between agencies and the other institutions of government—Congress, the Judiciary, and the President. Administrative law is important at every level of government—national, state, and local. With one exception, however, this book will discuss only federal administrative law. The exception is the discussion of due process in Chapter 3. Since the Due Process Clause of the U.S. Constitution applies to actions taken by agencies at all levels of government, the discussion of the influence of due process on agency decision-making procedures in Chapter 3 applies equally to agencies at every level of government. The discussion of administrative law in the rest of the book applies directly only to federal agencies. Knowledge of federal administrative law can be helpful to an understanding of state and local administrative law because state and local government institutions often borrow rules and doctrines from federal administrative law. There is so much variation among state and local administrative law systems, however, that it is dangerous to assume that a doctrine that is well entrenched in one jurisdiction exists in a similar form in another jurisdiction.

Congress has created hundreds of agencies over the two hundred and twenty years since the nation was founded. Some agencies have only limited powers. Thus, for instance, the powers of the Civil Rights Commission are limited to investigation, reporting, and publicizing. In some periods of time, the Civil Rights Commission has had a powerful influence on public opinion by investigating and exposing systematic racial discrimination, but it has never had the power to create or to change legal rights or to adjudicate disputes involving the rights of individuals.

In most contexts, however, when Congress creates an agency, it gives the agency a wide array of powers in its assigned area of responsibility, including the power to issue rules that have the same legally-binding effect as statutes and the power to issue final decisions in adjudicatory disputes that have effects indistinguishable from the effects of judicial decisions. In each of those cases, Congress concluded that an agency staffed by people with expertise in some specialized field would be able to do a better job than Congress in issuing rules of conduct in the agency's area of expertise and that the agency also would be able to do a better job than generalist judges in adjudicating disputes in its area of expertise. Some agencies, like the Federal Communications Commission (FCC) and the Environmental Protection Agency (EPA), have missions that are primarily regulatory in nature. Others, like the Social Security Administration (SSA) and the Center for Medicare and Medicaid Services (CMS), are primarily involved in implementation of benefit programs.

Most agencies perform myriad functions, including investigating, enforcing, reporting, record-keeping, and publicizing. The two most important agency functions are adjudicating and rulemaking. Agencies dominate both fields. Agencies adjudicate far more disputes involving the rights of individuals than all of the courts combined. Agencies also issue far more legally-binding general rules of conduct than Congress. Both of those functions have long taken place under a cloud of constitutional doubt, however.

The Supreme Court interprets Article I of the Constitution to confer on Congress the non-delegable power to make policy decisions that have legally-binding effects. From time-to-time, the Court has suggested that it might apply this non-delegation doctrine as the basis to hold unconstitutional a high proportion of the statutes that delegate rulemaking power to agencies. So far, however, the Court has only applied the non-delegation doctrine as the basis to hold invalid one extreme statute in 1935.

The Supreme Court also interprets Article III and the Seventh Amendment in ways that threaten the continued viability of much of the adjudicatory power of agencies. The Court sometimes interprets Article III to prohibit any institution except a court from adjudicating any dispute that involves what the Court calls "private rights," and the Court interprets the Seventh Amendment to prohibit any institution except a jury from resolving a factual dispute that arises in any controversy that was potentially the subject of a common law action in 1789. Taken to their logical extremes, those constitutional law doctrines have the potential to support holdings that a high proportion of the adjudicatory power now exercised by agencies is unconstitutional. So far, however, the Court has used those doctrines to invalidate only one adjudicatory system that was implemented by an institution other than an Article III court and/or a jury.

The history of the constitutional challenges to the rulemaking and adjudicatory powers of agencies is discussed in detail in Chapter 2. For now, it is sufficient to note that the challenges have been largely unsuccessful. There are three reasons to expect that they will continue to be largely unsuccessful. First, agency rulemaking and adjudication have long pedigrees. In 1789, the first Congress created the first agencies with the power to issue legally binding rules and the power to issue legally binding decisions in adjudicatory disputes. Second, agencies staffed by individuals with specialized expertise in their areas of responsibility and free to use relatively informal decision-making procedures are far better equipped than either overburdened legislative bodies or generalist judges to address problems that arise in implementing most regulatory or benefit programs. Third, it would simply be impossible for government to continue to perform the myriad functions it performs today without agencies that have the power to issue rules and to resolve adjudicatory disputes in their areas of expertise and statutory responsibility.

The Administrative Procedure Act[1] (APA) is to administrative law what the Constitution is to constitutional law. Congress enacted the APA in 1946, after over a decade of sharp debate,[2] in an effort to achieve uniformity with respect to agency decision-making procedures and the standards courts apply in reviewing agency actions. The APA has increased the degree of uniformity among agencies in both respects, but considerable variation still exists among agencies for two reasons.

First, some of the most important procedures required by the APA apply to an agency action only when the statute that authorizes the agency to take the action requires the agency to act "on the record after opportunity for agency hearing." Most agency-administered statutes do not include that requirement. Thus, an agency that is acting under a statute with an "on the record" requirement must use elaborate decision-making procedures—referred to as formal adjudication and formal rulemaking—while an agency that is acting under a statute that does not include those words need not use such elaborate formal procedures. Most agencies that conduct adjudicatory proceedings act under statutes that do not have an "on the record" requirement. Such an agency is free to use a procedure called informal adjudication. The APA requires an agency to provide few procedural safeguards when it engages in informal adjudication, so agencies adopt a wide variety of decision-making procedures that are tailored to the perceived needs of the type of adjudicatory disputes at issue. Second, Congress often adds mandatory procedures to the procedures required by the APA when

---

1. 5 U.S.C. §§ 551–706.

2. For an excellent discussion of the debates that led to passage of APA, see George Shepherd, Fierce Compromise: The Administrative Procedure Act Emerges from New Deal Politics, 90 Nw. U. L. Rev. 1557 (1996).

Congress authorizes an agency to take specific types of actions to implement specific agency-administered statutes. Thus, for instance, the APA requires an agency to use a simple three-step procedure when it issues a rule using the process referred to as informal rulemaking, but Congress has added several mandatory additional procedures when EPA issues a rule to implement the Clean Air Act. The differences between formal and informal adjudication are discussed in detail in chapter 3. The differences between formal and informal rulemaking are discussed in detail in chapter 4.

A lawyer who is called upon to answer an administrative law question should begin by reading the relevant provisions of the APA. The lawyer's task can not end with that step, however, for two reasons. First, some APA provisions apply to a class of agency actions only if the statute that authorizes the agency to act contains specific language, e.g., the "on the record" phrase discussed above, and some agency-administered statutes add to or modify the APA requirements otherwise applicable to a class of agency actions. Thus, the lawyer must read the statute that authorizes the agency action at issue simultaneously with the APA to understand the ways in which the statutes interact. Second, many APA provisions can bear several meanings, so the lawyer must read the opinions in the cases in which courts have interpreted each APA provision that appears to be relevant to the question.

When statutes do not provide clear answers to administrative law questions, courts often use an analogical reasoning process as an aid to decision-making. Thus, for instance, a court that is asked to determine what procedures an agency is required to use in a class of disputes or whether a relationship between an agency and another institution of government is permissible may characterize the class of agency actions at issue as "quasi judicial." The court will then refer to the procedures used by courts and the law governing the permissible relationships between courts, Congress, and the President to aid the court in its effort to identify the procedures the agency is required to use or the permissible relationships between the agency, Congress, and the President. Alternatively, a court might characterize a class of agency proceedings as "quasi-legislative," and then refer to the procedures Congress uses to enact a statute or the law governing the permissible relationships between Congress, the President, and the courts to assist the court in answering analogous questions about the procedures the agency must use or the permissibility of some relationship between the agency and another institution of government.

Courts use the analogical reasoning process with some frequency, and it is potentially useful for some purposes, but it also can lead a court astray. The analogy is never perfect. Agencies differ from both courts and legislative bodies in important ways even when they perform functions that are similar to those performed by courts or legislatures. In addition, the judicial and legislative functions are not the only potential sources of paradigms a court might use as an aid in deciding whether an agency decision-making process or an agency relationship with another government institution is acceptable. Over the last few decades, courts have begun to recognize that agencies are bureaucracies, and that there is a rich literature on bureaucracy that often can be valuable to a court in deciding whether an agency practice is permissible. As discussed in chapter 3, the norms and goals of bureaucratic decision-making differ in important ways from the norms and goals of judicial decision-making. Modern courts often borrow from the literature on bureaucratic justice, rather than the judicial model of justice, when they are called upon to decide whether an agency practice, procedure, or relationship with another institution of government is permissible.

When I describe the relationships between agencies and other government institutions, I often begin with a chart in which I place the three constitutionally-recognized branches of government—the President, the Congress, and the Courts—parallel to each other at the top, and then place agencies below the three branches, with a dotted line connecting each of the three branches with the agencies below them. The hierarchical relationship depicted on the chart reflects the fact that agencies are subservient to each of the three constitutionally-recognized branches. The dotted lines reflect the uncertain and variable relationships between agencies and the President, Congress, and the courts. The relationships are uncertain because the courts have not yet definitively resolved many of the questions concerning the constitutionally-permissible relationships between agencies and the three branches of government. The relationships are variable for two reasons. First, an institution may choose to create, or not to create, a particular relationship between it and an agency when the relationship is constitutionally permissible. Thus, for instance, it has always been permissible for the President to authorize an institution within the Executive Office of the President to review agency rules before they are issued in a final form, but no President created such a relationship until 1981. Second, some types of relationships are permissible in some contexts and not in others. Thus, for instance, the President can take an active role in attempting to persuade an agency to issue a rule

5

that is consistent with the President's policy preferences, but an attempt by a President to influence an agency decision in an adjudication would be inconsistent with Due Process in many circumstances.

Courts can rely on three sources of authority as their bases to require an agency to use a particular decision-making procedure—the Constitution, statutes, and the agency's own rules. (Of course, an agency can choose its own procedural rules within boundaries established by statutes and the Constitution, so an agency is bound by its own rules of procedure only until it chooses to amend those rules.) At one time, some courts believed that they also could rely on their inherent common law powers to justify a judicial decision that requires an agency to use procedures that the court considers necessary or desirable. In a landmark unanimous 1978 opinion, however, the Supreme Court held that a court cannot require an agency to use a procedure that is not required by the Constitution, a statute or an agency rule.[3] The Supreme Court made it clear that an agency has discretion to choose the procedures it wishes to use for various purposes as long as the agency remains within the sometimes broad range of procedural options made permissible by the Constitution and applicable statutes. That 1978 judicial decision was part of a general trend in the late 1970s and 1980s in which the Supreme Court instructed the lower courts to confer deference on many agency decisions.

3. Vermont Yankee Nuclear Power Corp. v. Natural Resources Defense Council, 435 U.S. 519 (1978).

Chapter Two

DELEGATION OF POWER TO AGENCIES

Most agencies have many powers, including the power to investigate, to prosecute, to require record-keeping and reporting, and to publicize. The most important agency powers, however, are the power to adjudicate disputes involving the rights of individuals and the power to issue legally-binding rules of conduct. Both of those agency powers have long existed under a cloud of constitutional doubt.

A. Constitutional Limits on the Power to Delegate Policymaking

Article I of the Constitution provides that "[a]ll legislative powers shall be vested in a Congress of the United States." For almost 200 years, the Court has interpreted that provision to prohibit Congress from delegating its legislative power and has equated legislative power with policymaking.[1] Thus, the non-delegation doctrine purports to prohibit Congress from delegating to agencies the power to make legally-binding policy decisions. The doctrine fits awkwardly in a legal system in which agencies make far more legally-binding policy decisions than Congress.

The non-delegation doctrine does not follow inevitably from the language of Article I. By its terms, the Constitution neither equates legislative power with policymaking nor prohibits Congress from delegating legislative power. Moreover, the first Congress enacted two statutes that delegated the power to make legally-binding policy decisions to other branches of government.[2] It seems unlikely that a Congress dominated by Framers of the Constitution would immediately act in a manner inconsistent with the Constitution. No Justice questioned the validity of the non-delegation doctrine until 2001, however, and a majority of the Court continues to reaffirm the doctrine.

The Court's application of the non-delegation doctrine has never coincided with its description of the doctrine. The Court has applied the doctrine to invalidate only one statute, and it has upheld many statutes that delegate to agencies the power to make

---

1. Brig Aurora, 11 U.S. 382 (1813); Marshall Field & Co. v. Clark, 143 U.S. 649, 692 (1892).

2. I Stat. 83 (1789); I Stat. 137 (1789).

legally-binding policy decisions. Shortly after the Court announced the non-delegation doctrine, it rejected constitutional challenges to statutes that appeared to violate the doctrine by describing the statutes as merely authorizing an agency to find the existence of a factual contingency that triggered application of a policy previously announced by Congress.[3] When that reasoning was no longer sufficient to allow the Court to uphold some statutes, the Court began to uphold statutes on the basis that Congress had made the important policy decisions and had authorized an agency only to "fill up the details."[4] When that reasoning was no longer sufficient to allow the Court to uphold some statutes, the Court began to uphold statutes that delegated policymaking power to an agency if the statute contained an "intelligible principle" that could limit an agency's policymaking discretion.[5] The Court has used that formulation of the non-delegation doctrine as the basis to uphold the validity of statutes that delegate policymaking power to agencies limited only by statutory standards that are devoid of substantive content, like "just and reasonable" and "public convenience and necessity."[6]

The one statute that the Court invalidated through application of the non-delegation doctrine was the National Industrial Recovery Act (NIRA). The Court issued two opinions in 1935 in which it held the critical provisions of NIRA unconstitutional.[7] NIRA was an extraordinary statute in which Congress delegated the power to determine the permissible output and pricing of virtually all goods to Boards that consisted of private parties who were major participants in the markets they were authorized to regulate. Many scholars and at least three Justices have since explained the Court's opinions that invalidated NIRA as based not on the principle that Congress cannot delegate policymaking power to a government agency but on the quite different principle that Congress cannot delegate broad regulatory power to private market participants with clear conflicts of interest.[8]

For decades after the Court held NIRA unconstitutional, the Court refused to apply the non-delegation doctrine to invalidate numerous statutes that delegated power as broadly as NIRA, and

3. Brig Aurora, 11 U.S. 382 (1813).

4. United States v. Grimaud, 220 U.S. 506, 517 (1911).

5. J.W. Hampton v. United States, 276 U.S. 394, 409 (1928).

6. E.g., Intermountain Rate Cases, 234 U.S. 476 (1914); St. Louis I.M. & S.R. Co. v. Taylor, 210 U.S. 281 (1908).

7. A.L.A. Schechter Poultry Corp. v. United States, 295 U.S. 495 (1935); Panama Refining Co. v. Ryan, 293 U.S. 388 (1935).

8. Clinton v. New York, 524 U.S. 417, 485 (1998) (Breyer, J., dissenting on behalf of three Justices).

most observers believed that the non-delegation doctrine was moribund. Some academics took a renewed interest in the doctrine in the 1970s, however. Several respected constitutional law scholars wrote books in which they argued that Congress was behaving in an irresponsible manner by refusing to resolve most policy disputes and by opting instead to delegate most policymaking to unelected agency decision-makers.[9] They urged the Court to reinvigorate the non-delegation doctrine. By 1980, it appeared that a majority of the Justices were prepared to do just that. Justice Rehnquist wrote an opinion in which he urged the Court to reinvigorate the non-delegation doctrine and argued that the Occupational Safety & Health Act (OSHA) violates the doctrine.[10] He asserted that the Constitution prohibits Congress from delegating major policy decisions to "politically unresponsive bureaucrats." A four-Justice plurality declined to join Justice Rehnquist's opinion, but the plurality attributed to Congress a substantive standard that Congress had not included in the statute and said that, in the absence of such a narrowing construction of the statute, they too would have to conclude that OSHA constituted an unconstitutional delegation of legislative power.[11]

No Justice has urged reinvigoration of the non-delegation doctrine since Justice Rehnquist argued that OSHA is unconstitutional, and the Court has unanimously upheld five broad delegations of policymaking power since then.[12] The Court has not fully explained its apparent abandonment of its short-lived attempt to reinvigorate the non-delegation doctrine, but many observers believe that the Court's unanimous 1984 opinion in Chevron v. Natural Resources Defense Council[13] provides two plausible explanations. In *Chevron*, the Court held that a reviewing court must uphold any reasonable agency construction of an ambiguous provision in an agency-administered statute. The Court reasoned that an agency decision to attribute a particular meaning to ambiguous language in an agency-administered statute is a policy decision. As such, it should be made by a politically-accountable institution. The Court went on to characterize a reviewing court as a politically-unaccountable institution, because federal judges are not elected and serve for life, and to characterize agencies as politically ac-

9. John Ely, Democracy and Distrust 132–34 (1980); James Freedman, Crisis and Legitimacy 93–94 (1978); Theodore Lowi, The End of Liberalism 93 (1969).

10. Industrial Union Dep't v. American Petroleum Institute, 448 U.S. 607, 686–87 (1980).

11. Id. at 646.

12. Whitman v. American Trucking Ass'ns, 531 U.S. 457 (2001); Loving v. United States, 517 U.S. 748 (1996); Touby v. United States, 500 U.S. 160 (1991); Skinner v. Mid–America Pipeline Co., 490 U.S. 212 (1989); Mistretta v. United States, 488 U.S. 361 (1989).

13. 467 U.S. 837.

countable institutions. The Court recognized that agency heads are not directly accountable to the public, but it characterized them as indirectly accountable to the public through the elected President, who has both the power to appoint them and the power to remove them from office. The Court said that it was appropriate for politically accountable agencies, rather than politically unaccountable judges, to make policy decisions within the scope of the power Congress delegated to them.

Chevron responded to Justice Rehnquist's argument in support of reinvigorating the non-delegation doctrine in two ways. First, it contradicted his assertion that agency decision-makers are "politically unresponsive bureaucrats" by recognizing that agency decision-makers are politically accountable through the President. Second, the deferential test the Court announced in *Chevron* provides an incentive for Congress to limit the policymaking power it confers on agencies. After *Chevron*, a member of Congress knows that any delegation of policymaking power to an agency actually is a delegation of power to Congress's political rival, the President. Many members of Congress do not want to delegate broad policymaking power to their political rival, the President, so they try to limit the scope of his discretionary power by limiting the scope of the power they delegate to agencies and by including in statutes that delegate power to agencies meaningful substantive limits on the exercise of that power. The Supreme Court's landmark opinion in *Chevron* is discussed in detail in chapter five.

The Court has explicitly acknowledged another reason for its apparent abandonment of the non-delegation doctrine. The Justices increasingly recognize that the non-delegation doctrine is impossible to implement in any principled and consistent manner. Thus, for instance, Justice Scalia said in 1989:

> Once it is conceded, as it must be, that no statute can be entirely precise, and that some judgments, even some judgments involving policy considerations, must be left to the officers executing the law and to the judges applying it, the debate over unconstitutional delegation becomes a debate not over a point of principle, but over a question of degree.... [I]t is small wonder that we have almost never felt qualified to second guess Congress regarding the permissible degree of policy judgment that can be left to those executing or applying the law.[14]

Two Justices no longer accept the principle that Congress can not delegate its legislative power. In 2001, Justices Souter and Stevens

14. Mistretta v. United States, 488 U.S. 361, 415–16 (1989).

expressed the view that Congress routinely and permissibly delegates legislative power to agencies.[15] It is always possible that the Court will resuscitate the non-delegation doctrine in response to some particularly egregious example of standardless delegation of vast policymaking power to an agency. For now, however, the doctrine seems to be moribund.

B. Constitutional Limits on the Power to Delegate Adjudication

Congress has been delegating adjudicatory power to agencies in a wide variety of contexts since 1789.[16] Yet, two provisions of the Constitution would seem to impose strict limits on the power of Congress to assign adjudicatory tasks to agencies. Article III provides that: "The judicial Power of the United States shall be vested in one Supreme Court, and in such lower courts as the Congress may from time to time ordain and establish." Agencies are not "courts," and adjudication is arguably an exercise of "the judicial Power." The Seventh Amendment provides that "the right of jury trial" "shall be preserved" in "suits at common law." At least some classes of agency adjudications arguably constitute "suits at common law," but no agency assigns fact-finding to a jury.

The Supreme Court has issued scores of opinions in which it has interpreted Article III and the Seventh Amendment in the process of attempting to reconcile those provisions of the Constitution with a system of government in which Congress assigns resolution of most adjudicatory disputes to tribunals that are not Article III courts and that do not use juries for fact finding. The result is not a clear and internally consistent body of law. Richard Fallon has engaged in a detailed analysis of the large and complicated body of case law that governs this conflict between the apparent intent of the Framers and the apparent preferences of Congress.[17] For present purposes, half a dozen opinions issued between 1932 and 1989 will suffice to provide an understanding of the legal framework within which such disputes are resolved and the important questions that the Court has not yet resolved in a clear and consistent manner.

---

15. Whitman v. American Trucking Ass'ns, 531 U.S. 457, 488–89 (2001).

16. E.g., I Stat. 137 (1789) (delegating to the President the task of awarding licenses to trade with the Indians). See also 12 The Papers of James Madison 265 (describing as "of a judiciary quality" task of resolving all disputes regarding claims against the Treasury that Congress delegated to Department of Treasury in 1789).

17. Richard Fallon, On Legislative Courts, Administrative Agencies and Article III, 101 Harv. L. Rev. 915 (1988).

For many years, the Court's 1932 opinion in Crowell v. Benson[18] was believed to provide a definitive means of reconciling Article III with assignment of adjudicatory power to agencies. The Court upheld the congressional assignment of power to adjudicate workers compensation disputes involving maritime workers to a federal agency even though courts previously resolved all such disputes through application of the common law of torts, Congress made only modest statutory changes to tort law when it reallocated adjudication of all such disputes from courts to an agency, and all such disputes were between two private parties rather than between a private party and the government.

The Court began by applying a long-standing distinction between public rights disputes that Congress can assign to non Article III tribunals and private rights disputes that must be adjudicated by Article III courts. The Court concluded that the workers compensation disputes at issue were private rights disputes because they had a common law antecedent that Congress left largely intact when it reallocated their adjudication to an agency and because they arose between two private parties rather than between the government and a private party. The Court went on, however, to uphold the reallocation of adjudication of workers compensation disputes to an agency because Article III courts would continue to play major roles in resolving such disputes. The Court referred to the availability of plenary review of the agency's decisions by an Article III court and emphasized particularly two doctrines that the Court was applying to all adjudicatory decisions issued by agencies at the time—the constitutional fact doctrine and the jurisdictional fact doctrine. Under those doctrines, a party who was dissatisfied with an adjudicatory decision issued by an agency was entitled to a de novo judicial trial of any contested issue of fact that had constitutional or jurisdictional implications.

The years that followed the Court's opinion in *Crowell* brought major changes in judicial review of agency adjudicatory decisions that tended to undermine the basis for the *Crowell* decision. As discussed in detail in section 3E, modern courts engage in highly deferential review of all aspects of agency decision-making, including agency findings of fact, and the Court long ago abandoned the constitutional and jurisdictional fact doctrines. With the exception of issues of fact that have First Amendment implications, courts apply the same deferential standard to review of agency findings of constitutional and jurisdictional facts that they do to other agency findings of fact. Those changes in administrative law doctrines

---

18.   285 U.S. 22 (1932).

raised doubts about the continuing viability of the holding and reasoning in *Crowell*.

The Court's 1982 decision in Northern Pipeline Const. Co. v. Marathon Pipe Line Co.[19] added to the pre-existing doubts about the continued validity of *Crowell* and cast a large shadow over the constitutionality of a high proportion of agency adjudicatory power. In *Northern Pipeline*, the Court held that the new system of adjudicating bankruptcy disputes Congress had created violated Article III by purporting to confer judicial power on the newly-created Article I bankruptcy courts. Congress had attempted to consolidate in a single forum—a bankruptcy court—resolution of all issues that arise in a bankruptcy proceeding, including interpretation of contracts between a bankrupt entity and its creditors. A four-Justice plurality reasoned that the statute was unconstitutional because (1) only an Article III court can adjudicate a private rights dispute, and (2) disputes concerning interpretation of contracts are private rights disputes because any dispute between individuals that had a common law antecedent is a private right dispute. The *Northern Pipeline* opinion cast doubt on the constitutionality of a high proportion of agency adjudicatory functions because many modern disputes that are adjudicated by agencies had common law antecedents. Thus, for instance, courts adjudicated many environmental disputes through application of the common law of nuisance before Congress assigned most environmental regulation to agencies, and economic regulation was implemented by courts long before Congress assigned that task to agencies.

Northern Pipeline was hard to interpret, however. There was no majority opinion. The conclusion of the plurality prevailed only because two Justices concurred in an opinion in which they expressed reservations about the breadth of the plurality opinion but did not state their own reasons for concluding that the statute was unconstitutional. Three Justices dissented on the basis that the Court was departing from its many precedents in which it had upheld statutes in which Congress had delegated power to adjudicate disputes among private individuals to agencies and to other non Article III tribunals subject to review by an Article III court.

The Court adopted a narrow interpretation of *Northern Pipeline* in the process of upholding another delegation of adjudicatory power to a non Article III tribunal in its 1985 decision in Thomas v. Union Carbide.[20] *Thomas* involved a challenge to a system of adjudication Congress created to resolve disputes about the value of

---

19.   458 U.S. 50 (1982).   **20.**   473 U.S. 568 (1985).

studies conducted by one firm to support its application to register a pesticide but used by another firm to support its application to register a similar pesticide. Congress believed that it would be efficient to allow one applicant to rely on another applicant's studies, but that it would be unfair (and arguably a violation of the Fifth Amendment prohibition on taking private property without just compensation) not to require the second firm to compensate the first firm for the value of the use of the studies done by the first firm. Congress instructed the agency that implements the licensing regime to convene arbitral panels to make binding determinations with respect to the money the second firm is required to pay the first firm to compensate it for the use of its studies.

In *Thomas*, a five-Justice majority rejected the Article III challenge to the system of binding arbitration Congress had authorized. The majority noted that the views expressed by the *Northern Pipeline* plurality had not been accepted by a majority, and it criticized those views for unnecessarily creating doubt about the validity of many adjudicatory systems implemented by agencies and other non Article III tribunals. The majority then described the public rights disputes that Congress can assign to non Article III tribunals in a manner that suggested that Congress can redesignate any class of previously private rights disputes as public rights disputes for pragmatic reasons. The four dissenting Justices adhered to the views they expressed when they constituted a plurality in *Northern Pipeline*.

The Court reaffirmed its narrow interpretation of *Northern Pipeline* the next Term in Commodity Futures Trading Commission v. Schor.[21] Congress created the Commodity Futures Trading Commission (CFTC) to issue rules governing the relationships between brokers and their customers and to adjudicate disputes with respect to compliance with those rules. CFTC encountered a serious problem in its efforts to adjudicate disputes about alleged rule violations by brokers. In a high proportion of cases, the broker who was the subject of a customer's complaint would file a counterclaim in which it alleged that the customer owed it money on account as a result of the same transactions that were the basis for the customer's complaint that it was the victim of rules violations by the broker. A jurisdictional dispute would then arise, since Congress did not give CFTC jurisdiction to adjudicate common law counterclaims filed by brokers, and it is at least arguable that Congress could not give CFTC power to adjudicate such disputes consistent with Article III. Brokers who filed common law counterclaims at

---

21.   478 U.S. 833 (1986).

CFTC and lost argued that CFTC lacked jurisdiction to adjudicate common law counterclaims.

As a formal legal matter, the jurisdictional arguments of the brokers had a solid foundation, but it would make no sense for CFTC to resolve disputes with respect to alleged violations of its rules and for courts to adjudicate the common law counterclaims that arise out of the same transactions that gave rise to the complaint that the broker injured the customer by violating CFTC rules. Such a bifurcation of adjudicatory responsibility would be massively inefficient and would lead to intractable problems attributable to conflicting findings of fact, applications of principles of collateral estoppel, and inevitable races to get either CFTC or a court to resolve the overlapping disputes first. CFTC responded to this problem by issuing a rule in which it asserted jurisdiction to resolve common law counterclaims filed by brokers. That led to a challenge to the constitutional validity of the CFTC rule as an arguable violation of Article III.

In *Schor*, a seven-Justice majority upheld the CFTC rule even though the majority acknowledged that common law counterclaims are private rights disputes. The majority rejected the formalistic approach the plurality took in *Northern Pipeline* in favor of a pragmatic and functional approach in which a court will uphold a congressional (or agency) decision to allocate adjudication of any discrete and limited class of disputes to an agency if Congress has good reasons to do so and includes safeguards of the rights of parties that are roughly equivalent to the safeguards a party would enjoy in a federal court. The majority referred to the characteristics of agency adjudications that make them roughly analogous to court adjudications and to the roles of Article III courts in reviewing agency adjudicatory decisions to insure that agencies comply with all applicable substantive and procedural rules.

The *Schor* majority also asserted that Schor had waived his Article III rights. Many scholars question the significance of the waiver theory, however, for three reasons. First, the Court upheld the adjudicatory regime in *Union Carbide* even in the absence of any arguable waiver. Second, it is unrealistic to expect a broker to assert his Article III right by passing up an opportunity to obtain prompt resolution of his counterclaim by CFTC. Third, it does not make sense to say that a private party can waive a provision of the Constitution that is designed to protect one Branch of government from incursions by another Branch. Two dissenting justices would have adhered to and applied the views expressed by the *Northern Pipeline* plurality.

After *Schor*, it appeared that the Court was willing to uphold any congressional decision to allocate any class of adjudicatory disputes to an agency if the class was not too large—arguably the fatal flaw in the bankruptcy statute that led to the Court's decision in *Northern Pipeline*—and if Congress gave good reasons for its decision to reallocate and accompanied its delegation of adjudicatory power with sufficient procedural safeguards and with a sufficient role for Article III courts to review the agency decisions. We could leave the discussion with that reasonably satisfactory description of the state of law if it were not for a subsequent decision in which a majority of the Court seemed to adopt and apply the highly formalistic approach of the *Northern Pipeline* plurality in interpreting and applying the Seventh Amendment.

Until 1989, the Court's decisions interpreting and applying the Seventh Amendment were consistent with its decision interpreting Article III in *Schor*. The most recent pre–1989 precedent was the Court's 1977 decision in Atlas Roofing Co. v. Occupational Safety and Health Review Commission.[22] Congress concluded that the pre-existing common law actions for negligence and wrongful death were inadequate to protect workers from occupational injuries, so it created a new agency-administered adjudicatory system in which an agency could impose civil penalties against a firm that causes an injury to an employee by creating an unsafe workplace. When the agency imposed penalties on Atlas, it argued that the Seventh Amendment precluded Congress from authorizing an agency acting without a jury to adjudicate disputes concerning workplace injuries because negligence and wrongful death actions were common law antecedents to the new statutory cause of action for civil penalties. The Court unanimously rejected that argument. The reasoning in the opinion was so broad that most people read it as an implicit invitation for Congress to replace many other pre-existing jury-administered adjudicatory systems with agency-administered adjudicatory systems. The Court concluded that the Seventh Amendment does not bar Congress from concluding that a pre-existing common law remedy is inadequate and replacing that remedy with an agency-administered remedy that is inherently incompatible with use of a jury to find facts.

In its 1989 opinion in Granfinanciera v. Nordberg, however, a six-Justice majority interpreted *Atlas* narrowly and returned to the formalistic approach used by the plurality in *Northern Pipeline* as its basis to interpret and apply the Seventh Amendment. The question was whether Congress could authorize bankruptcy courts operating without juries to adjudicate claims that a bankrupt entity

---

22.   430 U.S. 442 (1977).

had fraudulently conveyed something of value to keep it away from creditors. The majority reasoned that, while Congress can assign adjudication of a class of public rights disputes to an institution other than a jury, it cannot assign adjudication of a class of private rights disputes to an institution other than a jury if there was a common law antecedent to the private rights dispute at the time of the Framing of the Constitution. The majority concluded that a common law action for fraud would have been available to a plaintiff like the plaintiff in *Granfinanciera* at the time of the Framing and that such an action for fraud was a dispute involving private rights. Thus, the majority held that Congress could not assign the task of making findings of fact relevant to a bankruptcy/fraudulent conveyance dispute to any institution except a jury.

After the Court decided *Granfinanciera*, it is difficult, if not impossible, to provide any clear summary of the law in this area that is capable of explaining both the Court's most recent Article III decisions in *Union Carbide* and *Schor* and its most recent Seventh Amendment decision in *Granfinanciera*. The three dissenting Justices in *Granfinanciera* argued persuasively that those three decisions are inherently in conflict. Of course, it is important to remember that the Court has not held any agency adjudicatory system unconstitutional as a violation of either Article III or the Seventh Amendment. Both *Northern Pipeline* and *Granfinanciera* involved attempts by Congress to assign certain adjudicatory responsibilities to the Article I bankruptcy courts, though the reasoning in the opinions in each case would seem to apply to a congressional delegation of analogous adjudicatory power to an agency.

In a 2011 opinion, the Court suggested that it would not hold unlawful most, if any, adjudicatory systems implemented by agencies.[23] The question before the Court was whether Congress could reassign adjudication of a class of disputes from Article II courts to Article I bankruptcy courts. The dissenting Justices argued that it could and urged the Court to apply to all such cases the easy-to-meet test the Court applied in cases like *Schor* and *Union Carbide*. The majority applied instead the formalistic test the Court had applied in *Northern Pipeline* and held that the class of disputes could not be adjudicated by Article I bankruptcy courts. The majority distinguished cases "in which the claim at issue derives from a federal regulatory scheme, or in which resolution of the claim by an expert government agency is deemed essential to a limited regulatory objective within the agency's authority." The majority acknowledged that it was willing to apply the easy-to-meet test in those contexts.

23. Stern v. Marshall, __ U.S. __, 131 S.Ct. 2594 (2011).

Chapter Three

ADJUDICATION

A. Introductory Overview

There are three potential sources of procedures an agency must use in conducting an adjudication—the Due Process Clause of the Constitution, statutes, and the agency's own rules. Until 1978, some courts believed that they also had the power to require an agency to use additional procedures that are not required by the Constitution, statutes, or agency rules on the basis of a judicial determination that the additional procedures would improve the accuracy of the agency decision-making process or assist the court in its efforts to review the agency action. In 1978, however, the Supreme Court held unanimously that courts can only require an agency to use those procedures that are required by the Constitution, statutes, or agency rules.[1] The Court's decision arose in the context of a rulemaking, but the Court has since confirmed that its holding applies as well to agency adjudications.[2]

A lawyer who undertakes the task of determining the procedures an agency is required to use always should begin by reading the agency's own rules. The Supreme Court has held that an agency is required to comply with its own rules of procedure to the extent that those rules are intended to confer important rights on parties even if the rules go beyond the requirements of statutes and the Constitution,[3] and agencies often adopt rules of procedure that go beyond those requirements. The next logical step is to read the applicable statutes.

There are always two statutes that can be the source of procedural requirements applicable to an agency adjudication—the Administrative Procedure Act (APA) and the statute that authorizes the agency to take the particular adjudicatory action it is taking, often called the organic Act. Sections 554 through 558 of the APA describe elaborate procedures an agency must follow when

---

1. Vermont Yankee Nuclear Power Corp. v. NRDC, 435 U.S. 519, 546–48 (1978).

2. Pension Benefit Guaranty Corp. v. LTV Corp., 496 U.S. 633 (1990).

3. United States v. Nixon, 418 U.S. 683, 694–96 (1974); United States ex rel. Accardi v. Shaughnessy, 347 U.S. 260

(1954). An agency is not required to comply with a procedural rule that merely provides a means for the agency to conduct its business in an orderly manner, however. American Farm Lines v. Black Ball Freight Service, 397 U.S. 532 (1970).

it conducts an adjudication. As discussed in detail in section B, the procedures described in those sections of the APA resemble closely the procedures a court uses to adjudicate a dispute. Those procedures are often called formal adjudication.

APA section 554(a) makes the procedures described in sections 554 and 556–558 applicable only to adjudications conducted by an agency that is required by statute to conduct an adjudication "on the record after opportunity for agency hearing." Only a relatively small proportion of agency organic Acts have such a requirement. Most agency organic Acts require an agency only to conduct a "hearing" in an adjudication. Until 1972, many agencies and courts believed that a statutory requirement that an agency conduct a "hearing" had legal effects identical to the requirement that an agency act "on the record after opportunity for an agency hearing." Thus, courts often concluded that an agency that is required to conduct a hearing must use the formal trial-like procedures that courts use and that are described in APA sections 554 and 556–558. In two opinions handed down in 1972 and 1973, however, the Supreme Court held that "hearing" is ambiguous and that an agency often can satisfy the statutory requirement to conduct a hearing by using procedures that are much less formal than those used by a court or those described in APA sections 554 and 556–558.[4] Thus, for instance, the Court held that agencies had complied with the statutory requirement to conduct a hearing when they allowed interested parties to submit data and views in writing but did not allow the parties to present oral evidence or to cross-examine opposing evidence. Those cases were decided in the context of agency rulemakings, but circuit courts have since applied the holdings to adjudications.[5]

When the applicable agency organic Act does not contain the "on the record" requirement, an agency is not required to use formal adjudication. It is instead free to engage in what is often called informal adjudication. As discussed in detail in section C, an agency has a great deal of flexibility with respect to its choice of decision-making procedures when it engages in informal adjudication. The Supreme Court has held that only APA section 555 applies to an agency when it engages in informal adjudication.[6] That section is accurately labeled "Ancillary Matters." It does not

---

4. United States v. Florida East Coast Ry. Co., 410 U.S. 224 (1973); United States v. Allegheny–Ludlum Steel Corp., 406 U.S. 742 (1972).

5. E.g., Dominion Energy Brayton Point v. Johnson, 443 F.3d 12 (1st Cir. 2006); Chemical Waste Management v. EPA, 873 F.2d 1477 (D.C. Cir. 1989).

6. Pension Benefit Guaranty Corp. v. LTV Corp., 496 U.S. 633 (1990).

confer any important rights on participants in informal adjudications.

The organic Act that authorizes the agency to conduct the adjudication can be the source of procedural requirements in two ways. First, by including or excluding the words "on the record after opportunity for agency hearing," the organic Act determines whether the agency must use formal adjudication or can instead use informal adjudication. Second, the organic may itself impose various procedural requirements independent of the procedures described in the APA.

In the high proportion of adjudications in which an agency is free to use informal adjudication and in which its organic Act does not add other mandatory procedures, statutes provide no meaningful procedural safeguards. In some important classes of agency adjudications, however, the Due Process Clause requires an agency to provide at least some minimum procedural safeguards. The applicability and effects of the Due Process Clause are described in detail in section D. In addition, agencies often require by rule use of procedures that go well beyond those required by Due Process or by statutes because agencies themselves place a high value on both procedural fairness and maximizing accuracy in agency adjudicatory decision-making.

B. Formal Adjudication

When the statute the agency is implementing includes a provision that requires the agency to conduct adjudications "on the record after opportunity for agency hearing,"[7] APA sections 554 through 558 apply to the adjudications. Those sections require an agency to use procedures virtually identical to those used by a trial court, including (1) notice of legal authority and matters of fact and law asserted;[8] (2) an oral evidentiary hearing presided over by the agency, one of the members that comprise the agency, or an Administrative Law Judge (ALJ);[9] (3) the presiding officer may not communicate off the record with any party with respect to any contested substantive issue, or communicate with anyone in the agency who has an investigative or prosecutorial function;[10] (4) a party can be represented by an attorney or other authorized representative;[11] (5) the proponent of an order has the burden of proof;[12]

7. 5 U.S.C. § 554(a).
8. 5 U.S.C. § 554(b).
9. 5 U.S.C. § 556(b).
10. 5 U.S.C. §§ 554(b), 557 (d)(1).

11. 5 U.S.C. § 555(b).
12. 5 U.S.C. § 556(d).

(6) a party is entitled to present oral or documentary evidence;[13] (7) a party is entitled "to conduct such cross-examination as may be required for a full and true disclosure of the facts;"[14] (8) an order can be issued only on the basis of the record created at the hearing;[15] (9) a party is entitled to a transcript of evidence that is the exclusive record for decision;[16] and, (10) the decision must include "findings and conclusions, and the reasons or basis therefore, on all the material issues of fact, law, or discretion presented on the record."[17]

The role of the ALJ lies at the core of formal adjudication. The APA requires an agency that engages in formal adjudication to use one of three entities to preside at the oral evidentiary hearing—the agency, one of the members of the body that comprises the agency, or an ALJ.[18] It is highly impracticable for either the agency (e.g., the five members of the Federal Communications Commission) or a member of the agency (e.g., one of the five Commissioners) to preside at an oral evidentiary hearing, so agencies almost invariably designate an ALJ as the presiding officer. An ALJ is an employee of the agency at which he presides, but he[19] is almost as independent of the agency that employs him as a federal district judge is of the Executive and Legislative branches of government. Agencies are prohibited from evaluating the performance of ALJs, and the salary of each ALJ is determined through application of a rigid set of criteria by the Office of Personnel Management (OPM).[20] An agency can take no adverse action against an ALJ without conducting a formal adjudicatory proceeding at OPM at which the agency has the burden of proving that it has good cause to take the adverse action.[21] It is roughly as difficult for an agency to take adverse action against an ALJ as it is for the government to take adverse action against a life-tenured federal district judge. Agencies are required to assign ALJs to preside over cases by rotation, and an agency can omit an ALJ's Initial Decision in a case only if the ALJ becomes unavailable or the agency finds that "due and timely

---

13. 5 U.S.C. § 556(d).

14. 5 U.S.C. § 556(d).

15. 5 U.S.C. § 556(d).

16. 5 U.S.C. § 556(e).

17. 5 U.S.C. § 557(c)(3)(A).

18. 5 U.S.C. § 556(b).

19. ALJs are disproportionately males because the Office of Personnel Management is required by statute to award a large preference to military vet-

erans in determining who is eligible to be an ALJ, and military veterans are disproportionately males. A 1992 study found that 94% of ALJs are male. Paul Verkuil, Daniel Gifford, Charles Koch, Richard Pierce & Jeffrey Lubbers, The Federal Administrative Judiciary, II Reports and Recommendations of the Administrative Conference of the United States 1090 (1992).

20. 5 U.S.C. § 5372.

21. 5 U.S.C. § 3105.

execution of its functions imperatively and unavoidably so requires."[22]

ALJs perform functions that are analogous to the functions of federal district judges in most respects. The ALJ presides at the evidentiary hearing, makes all evidentiary rulings, and then issues a decision, called the Initial Decision, that includes findings with respect to all contested issues of fact, conclusions with respect to all issues of law, and reasoning that explains how the ALJ reasoned from the evidence to the findings and from the findings and conclusions to the ultimate decision.[23] The ALJ's role differs from that of a federal district judge in two critical respects, however.

First, and most important, an agency can replace an ALJ's Initial Decision, including his findings and conclusions, if it chooses to do so. In the words of the APA, "[o]n appeal from or review of the initial decision, the agency has all the powers which it would have in making the initial decision except as it may limit the issues on notice or by rule."[24] Moreover, the highly deferential substantial evidence test that reviewing courts apply to an agency finding of fact applies to the agency's finding, rather than to the ALJ's finding, even when the finding is based on an evaluation of the credibility of a witness and when the agency's finding is the opposite of the ALJ's finding.[25] This is in stark contrast to the limited and deferential role that circuit courts of appeal play in reviewing the decisions of federal district judges. It is justified by the superior subject matter expertise of the agency, vis a vis an ALJ, and by the need for the agency to maintain consistency, continuity, and coherence with respect to its decisions in large numbers of cases.

Second, the APA instructs ALJs to apply a short and simple standard in making all evidentiary rulings: "Any oral or documentary evidence may be received, but the agency as a matter of policy shall provide for the exclusion of irrelevant, immaterial, or unduly repetitious evidence." Moreover, an agency can rely on hearsay evidence that would not be admissible in a judicial trial as the agency's sole basis for a finding of fact even if the inadmissible hearsay evidence provides the only support for an agency finding and even if it is contradicted by the only evidence in the record that would be admissible in a judicial trial.[26] Thus, the rules of evidence that apply to formal agency adjudications are dramatically different

22. 5 U.S.C. §§ 557(b)(2), 557(d), 3105.

23. 5 U.S.C. §§ 556(c), 557(c).

24. 5 U.S.C. § 557(b).

25. See the detailed discussion of the substantial evidence test in § 3(E)(2).

26. Id.

from the long and complicated Federal Rules of Evidence (FRE) that apply to trials conducted in federal district courts.[27] That difference can be explained by the absence of juries in agency adjudications. The FRE are specifically designed to assure fairness in the unique context of conducting a jury trial. No other system of civil justice in the world, including the U.S. administrative system of justice, has evidence rules that even remotely resemble the FRE because no other system of justice uses juries to resolve most disputes.

C.   Informal Adjudication

Until 1972, most agencies and courts believed that an agency was required to use the elaborate procedures required for formal adjudication when the agency was required by statute to conduct a "hearing" to adjudicate a class of disputes. That understanding was undermined by a pair of Supreme Court opinions issued in 1972 and 1973. In those opinions, the Court surprised many participants in the administrative justice system by holding that "hearing" is an ambiguous term, and that the statutory requirement to conduct a hearing often can be satisfied by providing parties to a proceeding the opportunity to present evidence and views solely in written form.[28]

Initially, that pair of opinions produced a split among the circuits with respect to the meaning of "hearing" in the context of adjudications. The two Supreme Court cases involved rulemaking proceedings, rather than adjudications. In each case, the agency was deciding whether to issue a general rule of conduct to address a problem, rather than resolving a dispute between individuals. Moreover, the contested facts in each case involved pure issues of "legislative fact"—in order to decide what kind of rule to issue, the agency resolved disputes with respect to the kinds of general facts that typically form the basis for legislative action, such as the reasons why a severe rail car shortage arose during the grain harvesting season in the midwest each year and the best method of changing the regulation of railroads to avoid recurrence of that

---

27. There is one important exception to this generalization. The rules governing evidentiary privileges apply equally in agency adjudications because they are designed to protect relationships that would be damaged as much by invasion of the privilege in an agency proceeding as by its invasion in a judicial trial. For detailed discussion of the difference between the rules of evidence that apply in judicial proceedings and the rules that apply in agency proceedings, see Richard Pierce, Use of the Federal Rules of Evidence in Federal Agency Adjudications, 39 Admin. L. Rev. 1 (1987).

28. United States v. Florida East Coast Ry. Co., 410 U.S. 224 (1973); United States v. Allegheny–Ludlum Steel Corp., 406 U.S. 742 (1972).

annual crisis. Courts and commentators have long distinguished between such legislative fact disputes and disputes with respect to adjudicative facts—the kinds of specific facts with respect to individuals and past events that juries usually are called upon to resolve in court trials.[29]

For about fifteen years after the Court held that the statutory requirement of a "hearing" could be satisfied by a written exchange of data and views in the context of a rulemaking, about half of circuit courts applied that holding to adjudications as well, while the other half distinguished the adjudicative process from the rulemaking process and held that an agency must use formal adjudication when it adjudicates a dispute that involves disputed issues of adjudicative fact under a statute that requires the agency to conduct a "hearing." Thus, for instance, the First Circuit held that the Environmental Protection Agency (EPA) was required to use formal adjudication when it decided whether to issue a discharge permit under the Clean Water Act if the applicant alleged that issuance of the permit would cause either no harm to the environment or an amount of harm that is permissible under the statute and opponents alleged that issuance of the permit would cause a legally impermissible level of harm to the environment.[30]

Landmark unanimous Supreme Court opinions issued in 1978 and 1984 eventually eliminated that split among the circuits and convinced circuit courts to hold that an agency is not required to use formal adjudication when it adjudicates a dispute under a statute that requires the agency to conduct a hearing. The first was Vermont Yankee Nuclear Power Corp. v. Natural Resources Defense Council,[31] in which the Court held that a reviewing court can reverse an agency action for failure to provide a procedural safeguard only if the safeguard is required by agency rule, statute, or the Constitution. That decision ended the practice of some circuit courts of requiring an agency to conduct an oral evidentiary hearing when the court believed that such a hearing was necessary or desirable in circumstances in which the agency was not required by rule, statute, or the Constitution to conduct such a hearing.

The second was Chevron v. Natural Resources Defense Council, in which the Court instructed lower courts to uphold agency interpretations of ambiguous provisions in agency-administered statutes as long as the interpretation is reasonable.[32] Once the

---

29. Kenneth Davis, An Approach to Problems of Evidence in the Administrative Process, 55 Harv. L. Rev. 364 (1942).

30. Seacoast Anti–Pollution League v. Costle, 572 F.2d 872 (1st Cir. 1978).

31. 435 U.S. 519 (1978).

32. 467 U.S. 837 (1984). *Chevron* is discussed in detail in Chapter Five.

Court decided *Chevron*, circuit courts that had previously held that an agency must use formal adjudication when its statute requires it to provide a "hearing" in an adjudication were required to reconsider those holdings in light of the new framework for judicial review announced in *Chevron*. In each case, the circuit court concluded that it was required to uphold an agency decision to abandon the use of formal adjudication and to substitute a less formal procedure such as a written exchange of data and views when the agency was required to provide a hearing.[33] Each court noted that the Supreme Court had previously held that "hearing" was ambiguous in its 1972 and 1973 opinions, so a court could reject an agency interpretation of the term "hearing" to refer to only a written exchange of data and views only if the court could conclude that such an agency interpretation is unreasonable.

It is conceivable that a court might some day reject such an agency interpretation of "hearing" as unreasonable in a particular context. A court might conclude that an agency was unreasonable if it interpreted "hearing" to allow the agency to resolve disputes with respect to adjudicative facts that raise serious credibility issues without conducting some kind of oral evidentiary hearing. Agencies that implement benefit systems are sometimes required to resolve factual disputes of that type, and the Supreme Court has attached great significance to the availability of oral testimony and cross-examination in cases of that type.[34] So far, however, the cases in which circuit courts have been called upon to decide whether an agency interpretation of hearing is reasonable have arisen in the contexts of economic, environmental, health, and safety regulation. Courts and agencies have come increasingly to recognize that written exchanges of data and views provide at least as good a basis as oral evidentiary hearings to resolve the kinds of factual disputes that arise in regulatory adjudications, and that such a "paper hearing" can be completed in a small fraction of the time required to conduct an oral evidentiary hearing.

Few agencies are required to conduct adjudications "on the record after opportunity for agency hearing," so few are required to engage in formal adjudication. The vast majority of agencies are free to use informal adjudication to resolve all of the adjudicatory disputes that come before them. An agency that can use informal adjudication to resolve a class of disputes typically has great discretion in choosing the procedures it makes available. There are four

---

33. E.g., Dominion Energy Brayton Point v. Johnson, 443 F.3d 12 (1st Cir. 2006); Chemical Waste Management v. EPA, 873 F.2d 1477 (D.C. Cir. 1989).

34. See cases discussed in § 3(D)(2).

potential sources of limits on an agency's procedural discretion when it engages in informal adjudication, and each has only limited effects.

First, some agency adjudicatory decisions are subject to the Due Process Clause. In such cases, judicial interpretations of Due Process provide a floor on the procedures the agency can use. As discussed in detail in the next section of this chapter, however, Due Process applies to only a fraction of agency adjudications and, when it applies, is usually establishes a procedural floor so low that the agency still enjoys considerable discretion with respect to its choice of decision-making procedures. Second, the APA requires an agency to provide some procedural safeguards in an adjudication, but they are de minimis.[35] Third, in theory, the statute that authorizes the agency to conduct a class of adjudications can require the agency to use specific procedures, but most such statutes do not go beyond ambiguous requirements such as the requirement that the agency conduct a hearing. Fourth, agency rules provide a source of judicial-ly-enforceable procedures to the extent that they confer valuable procedural rights on parties, but, of course, agencies are free to choose their own rules of procedure except to the extent that the Constitution or statutes limit that freedom.

Agency procedures for conducting informal adjudications vary on a long spectrum from proceedings that incorporate all or most of the elaborate procedures required in a formal adjudication, to the "paper hearings" that have become common in many regulatory contexts, to extremely brief and informal meetings. This wide range of procedures should not be surprising when you remember that federal agencies adjudicate millions of disputes per year and that those adjudications arise in an extraordinarily wide range of circumstances. An empirical study found that most agencies provide at least four procedural safeguards: (1) notice of issues presented; (2) an opportunity to present data and arguments in either written or oral form; (3) a decision by a neutral decision-maker; and, (4) a statement of reasons for the decision.[36] Many agencies provide oral

35. In Pension Benefit Guaranty Corp. v. LTV Corp., 496 U.S. 633 (1990), the Court held that only APA § 555 applies to an informal adjudication. That section authorizes a person who is compelled to appear before an agency to retain an attorney to accompany him, limits an agency's ability to require a report or other investigative act to circumstances in which the requirement is authorized by law, authorizes a person who provides a statement, data, or report to an agency to obtain a copy of the statement, data, or report, limits the issuance of subpoenas to circumstances in which there has been a showing of general relevance and reasonable scope, and requires an agency to provide a prompt notice of denial of any written request, accompanied by a brief explanation of the grounds for denial.

36. Paul Verkuil, A Study of Informal Adjudication Procedures, 43 U. Chi. L. Rev. 739 (1976).

evidentiary hearings that are analogous to those required in formal adjudication with one critical exception. Most agencies that are not required to use ALJs to preside in adjudications choose to hire other people to perform those functions. Non–ALJ adjudicatory decision-makers have many different titles at different agencies, but they are often referred to as Administrative Judges (AJs). AJs outnumber ALJs by a factor of over two-to-one, and the proportion of disputes that are resolved by AJs is increasing, primarily because ALJs are far more expensive than most AJs, and because agencies have no means of applying productivity and quality controls to their ALJs.[37]

D.   Influence of Due Process

Judicial applications of the Due Process Clause can influence agency choices of decision-making procedures in several ways. A judicial decision that applies the Due Process Clause as the basis for a holding that an agency must provide specified minimum procedural safeguards has an obvious direct effect on the agency. But judicial applications of the Due Process Clause can have powerful indirect effects as well. Agencies that have not been the subject of a due process challenge to their decision-making procedures study judicial decisions involving agencies with arguably analogous adjudicative functions in an effort to choose decision-making procedures that are likely to withstand such a challenge in the future. Even agencies with adjudicatory functions that do not fall within the scope of the Due Process Clause may use judicial decisions that apply the Due Process Clause to other agencies as an aid in choosing their own procedures. An agency often will take this approach either because it believes that a court is likely to use similar reasoning in deciding whether the agency's interpretation of a an ambiguous term like "hearing" is reasonable, and thus should be upheld, or because the agency is persuaded by the reasoning of the courts that the procedures the courts require in arguably analogous contexts will further the agency's own interests in improving the accuracy of its decision-making process. Thus, judicial applications of the Due Process Clause influence agency choices of procedures in many ways.

1.   *Scope of Due Process*

The first logical step in identifying the procedures required by due process is to determine whether the Due Process Clause applies

---

37. See The Federal Administrative Judiciary, cited in note 19, supra.

at all to the decision-making process at issue. This is a multi-step process that begins by distinguishing between government actions that affect an identified individual based on characteristics unique to the individual and government actions that affect a group or class of individuals. A pair of Supreme Court opinions issued at the beginning of the twentieth century continue to govern this process of distinction. In Londoner v. Denver,[38] the Court held that the City of Denver was required by due process to provide a property owner some kind of hearing before it could determine that his property had increased in value, and thus that the owner owed increased taxes, due to a street paving project. A few years later, however, in Bi–Metallic Investment Co. v. State Board of Equalization,[39] the Court held that a property owner was not entitled to any kind of hearing before the State imposed an across-the-board increase in property taxes on the owner. The Court reasoned that:

> Where a rule of conduct applies to more than a few people it is impracticable that every one should have a direct voice in its adoption. The Constitution does not require all public acts to be done in town meeting or an assembly of the whole. General statutes within the state power are passed that affect the person or property of individuals, sometimes to the point of ruin, without giving them a chance to be heard.... There must be limit to individual argument in such matters if government is to go on.

In other words, if the government acts in a manner that harms you as an individual based on characteristics unique to you or your conduct, you may be able to invoke the judicial process, in the form of a judicial opinion interpreting and applying the Due Process Clause, to protect you from potential arbitrary or unjustified action. However, if the government acts in a manner that hurts you in your capacity as a member of a group or class of individuals, your recourse is not to the judicial process, but to the political process— you can complain to your elected representatives or seek their replacement at the next election. The Court uses the *Londoner/Bi– Metallic* distinction as a short-hand way of saying that, while the Due Process Clause may apply to an agency adjudicative decision, it rarely applies to an agency rulemaking proceeding because agency rules rarely single out an individual for adverse treatment, but instead apply to an entire class of individuals.

Due process does not apply to all agency adjudications. It applies only when the government "deprives" a person of "life,"

---

38.   210 U.S. 373 (1908).   **39.**   239 U.S. 441 (1915).

"liberty," or "property." No agency has the power to deprive anyone of life, so the Due Process Clause can apply to an agency adjudicative decision only if it deprives a person of property or liberty. Until 1970, the court defined property to refer only to state-recognized forms of common law property, e.g., your house, your car, etc. and to professional licenses that a person obtained through the sweat of her brow, e.g., your license to practice law. If a person claimed to have a property interest in a government benefit, a court would call it a mere privilege that does not qualify as property. Similarly, if a person claimed that a government contract created a property interest, a court would scoff at the claim and refer the person to the well-recognized distinction between property rights and contract rights. That situation changed dramatically as a result of a pair of Supreme Court opinions issued in 1970 and 1972.

In Goldberg v. Kelly,[40] a person who had been receiving a welfare benefit, Aid to Families with Dependent Children (AFDC), argued that she had been deprived of property without due process of law because the New York City welfare department had not provided her sufficient process before it decided that she was no longer entitled to receive AFDC benefits and terminated her payments. Instead of contesting the individual's argument, the government conceded the point on the basis of two articles in which a Yale law professor had argued that a modern capitalist economy inevitably produces some poverty and, thus, that the courts should recognize welfare benefits as a form of property.[41] A six-Justice majority accepted that argument and held that AFDC benefits "are a matter of entitlement for persons qualified to receive them." Thus, if a statute is written in a manner that creates a conditional entitlement, e.g., "if you have the following characteristics, you are entitled to the following benefit," and if a person has been receiving the benefits described by the statute based on a determination that the person is eligible, the person has a property interest in the benefits that cannot be deprived by the government without due process of law.

In Perry v. Sindermann,[42] the Court held that a person who has a contractual right to retain his government job unless he is terminated for cause, commonly referred to as tenure, has a property interest in his job that cannot be deprived without due process of

---

40. 397 U.S. 254 (1970).

41. Charles Reich, Individual Rights and Social Welfare: The Emerging Legal Issues, 74 Yale L. J. 1245 (1965); Charles Reich, The New Property, 73 Yale L. J. 733 (1964).

42. 408 U.S. 593 (1972). But see Board of Regents v. Roth, 408 U.S. 564 (1972) (untenured government employee, i.e., employee who can be fired at will, has no property interest in his job).

law. Between them, *Goldberg* and *Perry* probably increased the scope of the property interests that are within the scope of due process protection at least a hundred-fold.

The Court's decisions to expand the scope of property to include statutory entitlements and the jobs of tenured government employees have met with considerable criticism. Thus, for instance, a student Note in Columbia Law Review[43] argued that it made no sense to say that contracts create property rights for constitutional purposes when the Framers used each term in different parts of the Constitution for different purposes and obviously knew that property rights and contract rights differed significantly. Moreover, if government contracts create property rights, it makes no sense to draw the line in such a way as to include employment contracts but to exclude contracts for paper clips or jet fighters. So far, however, the Court has adhered to its holding in *Perry*, and no court has extended that holding to cover government contracts other than employment contracts.

Justice (later Chief Justice) Rehnquist spent decades attempting to persuade his colleagues to use a back door technique to overrule *Goldberg* and to eliminate statutory benefits from the definition of property. Justice Rehnquist argued that a party who relies on a statute as the source of a property right must accept "the bitter with the sweet."[44] In other words, if a person wants to use a statute to establish the intent of the legislature to confer on the person a statutory right with a particular substantive scope, the person must accept the procedural scope of the right as well. Thus, if a statute creates a substantive right in one provision and includes another provision that describes the procedures through which an agency can terminate the right, a court must give effect to both provisions of the statute. For a while, it appeared that at least a plurality, and perhaps a majority, of Justices accepted that method of reasoning.[45] In a 1985 opinion, however, an eight-Justice majority rejected Justice Rehnquist's theory and held that "the categories of substance and procedure are distinct."[46] Thus, once a court determines that a legislative body has created a property right by describing a government benefit in the form of a conditional entitlement, it is up to a court to determine the process the government

43. Note, Breach of Contract as a Due Process Violation: Can the Constitution be a Font of Contract Law? 90 Colum. L. Rev. 1098 (1990).

44. Arnett v. Kennedy, 416 U.S. 134 (1974).

45. Bishop v. Wood, 426 U.S. 341 (1976).

46. Cleveland Board of Education v. Loudermill, 470 U.S. 532 (1985).

must provide to deprive a person of that property right through judicial application of the Due Process Clause.

Before 1971, liberty was also defined narrowly for due process purposes. The Court applied it only to literal restraints on liberty, like incarceration or involuntary commitment, and to freedom to exercise constitutional rights. In a 1971 opinion, the Court seemed to expand the scope of the liberty interests protected by due process dramatically. It held that a person who had been named an alcoholic in a list distributed by a local government to inform liquor store owners not to sell alcohol to the listed individuals had been deprived of his liberty interest in the form of his right to be free from official stigmatization.[47] In a 1976 opinion, however, the Court distinguished its 1971 decision and held that a person who was officially labeled a shoplifter had not been deprived of a liberty interest.[48] The Court characterized its 1971 opinion as creating something called the "stigma plus" test, that recognizes a deprivation of a liberty interest when the government simultaneous stigmatizes a person and deprives that person of something tangible. The Court made it clear that the tangible something of which the person is deprived need not itself qualify as a protected property interest. The Court said that the deprivation of the alleged alcoholic's right to purchase alcohol qualified as the "plus" for purposes of the stigma plus test in the factual context in which the Court originally recognized a liberty interest in freedom from official stigmatization in 1971.

The Court has applied the stigma plus test as a source of liberty interests since 1976. The test has an unfortunate effect in the context in which it is used most frequently. If a government agency terminates an at will employee without giving a reason or with a stated reason that is relatively bland, the agency has not deprived the person of either a property right or a liberty right, so the agency can act without using any constitutionally-required procedures. If, however, an agency terminates an at will employee for engaging in serious misconduct, e.g., theft or sexual misconduct, the termination qualifies as stigma plus, and the agency cannot act without providing procedures that are expensive, time-consuming, and often embarrassing to the agency. In this legal environment, agencies that discover that an untenured employee has engaged in serious misconduct often terminate the employee without giving any reason or by giving a bland and disingenuous reason. This common practice, referred to as "passing the trash" by public school officials and other agency personnel managers, often has the

---

47. Wisconsin v. Constantineau, 400 U.S. 433 (1971).

48. Paul v. Davis, 424 U.S. 693 (1976).

effect of allowing an abusive school teacher or a dishonest clerk to remain in government service for many years.

Courts differ in their interpretations of the actions that qualify as a "deprivation" of a property interest for due process purposes. Some courts conclude that a person has been deprived of a property interest in the form of a statutory entitlement to a government benefit if the person claims to be eligible for the benefit and was denied the benefit even if the person was never previously determined to be eligible for the benefit and never previously received the benefit.[49] Other courts conclude that a person was deprived of a property interest only if the person was previously determined to be eligible for the benefit and was actually receiving the benefit before the agency decided that the person was no longer eligible for the benefit.[50] The Supreme Court has not yet resolved this dispute among circuit courts.

2. *Procedures Required by Due Process*

If a court determines that an agency has deprived a person of an interest in property or liberty in an adjudication, the court must then identify the minimum procedures the agency is required to use to satisfy due process. For this purpose, courts apply the three-part social cost-benefit test the Supreme Court announced in its landmark 1976 opinion in Mathews v. Eldridge:

"[D]ue process," unlike some legal rules, is not a technical conception with a fixed content unrelated to time, place and circumstances. . . . [I]dentification of the specific dictates of due process generally requires consideration of three distinct factors: First, the private interest that will be affected by the official action; second, the risk of an erroneous deprivation of such interest through the procedures used, and the probable value, if any, of additional or substitute procedural safeguards; and finally, the Government's interest, including the function involved and the fiscal and administrative burdens that the additional or substitute procedural requirement would entail.[51]

The *Mathews* test is difficult to apply and can produce a wide range of outcomes. Thus, for instance, the Court held that the

49. E.g., Purisch v. Tennessee Technological University, 76 F.3d 1414 (6th Cir. 1996) (untenured employee had a property interest in a fair process for deciding whether to grant the employee tenure.)

50. E.g., Kyle v. Morton High School, 144 F.3d 448 (7th Cir. 1998) (untenured employee had no property interest in her claim that she should have been granted tenure.)
51. 424 U.S. 319, 335 (1976).

government cannot deprive a person of AFDC benefits without first conducting an oral evidentiary hearing,[52] but the Court held that the government can deprive a person of social security disability benefits based on a pre-deprivation written exchange of data and views followed by a post-deprivation opportunity to obtain an oral evidentiary hearing,[53] and the Court held that a public school student can be suspended based solely on a brief contemporaneous informal meeting with a school official at which the student has the opportunity to provide his side of the story.[54] The test is so malleable and so dependent on the values each judge or Justice attaches to the three factors a court is required to consider that it often produces five-to-four decisions and sometimes even produces a three-way division among the Justices.[55]

The contrasting opinions of the Court in two of its most famous due process cases illustrate the nature of the three-part *Mathews* test. In *Goldberg*,[56] the Court confronted a constitutional challenge to the procedures then-used by the New York City (NYC) welfare agency to decide whether an individual is no longer eligible to receive AFDC payments. AFDC was a federally-funded but locally-administered welfare program. The statute was written in the form of a conditional entitlement, i.e, if you have the following characteristics, you are entitled to the following benefits. The eligibility criteria for AFDC benefits were complicated in their details, but generally the relatively modest benefits were available to a mother of young children who had virtually no assets and no husband or other regular male companion who was capable of providing support to her children.

At the time the Court decided *Goldberg*, the NYC welfare agency added an applicant to the list of those eligible to receive AFDC payments relatively quickly after only a brief effort to check the accuracy of the facts alleged in the individual's application. In some cases, the agency later discovered information that suggested that the individual was not eligible at the time the agency added her name to the list of recipients of AFDC benefits (or later became ineligible) because, for instance, she had a husband or other regular male companion who was able to provide support to her children. In such a case, the agency first conducted an ex parte investigation

---

52. Goldberg v. Kelly, 397 U.S. 254 (1970).

53. Mathews v. Eldridge, 424 U.S. 319 (1976).

54. Goss v. Lopez, 419 U.S. 565 (1975).

55. See, e.g., Brock v. Roadway Express, 481 U.S. 252 (1987) (Justices di-

vide three ways in identifying the procedures an agency must use when it orders a firm to rehire an employee through application of a whistleblower statute.)

56. 397 U.S. 254 (1970).

in an effort to verify or refute the relevant facts. If the agency was persuaded that the individual was not eligible, the agency then sent the individual a notice in which it informed her of the agency's preliminary finding and the bases for that preliminary finding and gave her a specified period of time in which to submit such written evidence of her eligibility for AFDC benefits as she chose to submit. If the agency determined that the individual was ineligible based on consideration of the evidence the agency had gathered from other sources and the written materials submitted by the individual, the agency notified the individual of its determination, immediately removed her from the list of individuals eligible to receive AFDC benefits, and notified her that she could obtain an oral evidentiary hearing to contest the agency's determination by requesting such a hearing. Of course, it took a while to obtain a decision as a result of such a hearing, so an individual who was determined to be ineligible as a result of the agency's pre-termination consideration of the written information provided by the individual but who was later determined to be eligible as a result of the agency's post-termination consideration of the evidence adduced at the oral hearing received no AFDC benefits for approximately a year.

When Kelly was notified that the agency had determined that she was ineligible for AFDC benefits and that her benefits were being terminated immediately, she decided to challenge the constitutional adequacy of the procedures used to decide that she was ineligible rather than to avail herself of the opportunity for the post-termination oral evidentiary hearing the agency offered her. A six-Justice majority of the Supreme Court first held that AFDC benefits are "property" within the scope of the Due Process Clause and then held that the procedures the agency made available to make eligibility decision were not sufficient to satisfy due process. The Court held that an agency can not terminate AFDC benefits to an individual who claims to be entitled to those benefits without providing the individual a pre-termination oral hearing, including the right to cross-examine any witnesses who testify that the individual is not eligible.

Six years later, the Court reached a dramatically different result in a case that seemed to many observers to be remarkably similar to *Goldberg*. In Mathews v. Eldridge,[57] the Court confronted a challenge to the constitutional adequacy of the procedures that the Social Security Administration (SSA) was using to decide whether an individual who had previously been determined to be eligible for disability benefits and who had been receiving such

---

57. 424 U.S. 319 (1976).

benefits was, in fact, ineligible for continued receipt of disability benefits. SSA was using procedures identical to the procedures that the Court had held to be inadequate in the AFDC context. If SSA made a preliminary determination that an individual was not eligible for disability benefits based on an ex parte investigation, SSA would notify the individual of that preliminary determination and the basis for it and would provide the individual a specified period of time in which to provide any written materials the individual chose to submit to demonstrate that the individual is eligible for disability benefits. If SSA determined that the individual was ineligible based on its consideration of the evidence it had gathered from other sources and the written material provided by the individual, SSA notified the individual that he was no longer eligible and that his benefits had been terminated. The notice also informed the individual that he had a right to a post-termination oral evidentiary hearing if he decided to contest the validity of the determination the agency had made on the basis of its pre-termination consideration of the written materials the individual had submitted. The Court held that social security disability benefits qualify as property for due process purposes but that the procedures used by SSA were adequate to satisfy due process.

In *Mathews,* a majority of the Court announced the three-part balancing test that courts have applied ever since to determine the minimum procedures an agency must use and then distinguished the Court's holdings in *Goldberg* and *Mathews* by reference to that test. The Court identified three distinguishing features that it found to be outcome-determinative. First, while an AFDC beneficiary who has her benefits wrongfully terminated is in an "immediately desperate situation" because she and her children have been deprived of "the very means by which to live," a social security disability beneficiary who has his benefits wrongfully terminated is not necessarily in such a terrible situation because disability benefits are not means-tested and, thus, many disability beneficiaries will have access to some other means of support. That distinction relates to the first part of the balancing test—the importance of "the private interest that will be affected by the official action."

Second, the Court distinguished between the issues that are most frequently contested in AFDC cases and the issues that are most frequently contested in disability cases. It characterized the issues in a typical disability dispute as relatively objective because they involve an individual's health state, while it characterized the issues in a typical AFDC dispute as relatively subjective because they focus on an individual's patterns of behavior, e.g., is the beneficiary living with a man who is capable of supporting her children? The Court observed that witness veracity is more important in resolving a typical AFDC dispute than in resolving a typical disability dispute and that opportunity to observe a witness's demeanor and opportunity to cross examine a witness are more important in disputes that raise veracity concerns. The second distinction drawn by the Court relates to the second part of the test—"the risk of an erroneous deprivation ... through the procedures used, and the probable value, if any, of additional or substitute procedures."

The third distinguishing feature identified by the Court also related to the second part of the test. The Court noted that the AFDC beneficiaries who are the primary participants in AFDC eligibility proceedings usually have limited educations that make it difficult for them to participate effectively in written proceedings. By contrast, the Court stated that doctors are the primary participants in disability eligibility proceedings, and it noted that doctors typically have a well-developed ability to express themselves in writing.

The three distinguishing features identified by the *Mathews* Court continue to be important in due process decision-making. In particular, the more important a court considers the interest at stake in a class of disputes the more likely it is to require the agency to use expensive and time-consuming procedures to resolve the class of disputes, and the more important the court considers questions of witness veracity to be in a class of disputes the more likely the court is to require the agency to provide an opportunity for an oral evidentiary hearing. Many scholars believe that the *Mathews* Court also was influenced by other unstated factors, however. There are many reasons for that belief.

First, while each of the distinctions the Court identified has some basis, it would be easy to make too much of each of those distinctions. Thus, for instance, while the typical disability beneficiary is somewhat better off financially than the typical AFDC beneficiary, most disability beneficiaries also would find themselves in an extremely difficult financial situation if they were the subject of an erroneous determination of ineligibility. Similarly, while the issues disputed most often in disability cases are somewhat more objective than the issues that are disputed most often in AFDC cases, most contested disability disputes involve disputes that often elicit different opinions from equally able doctors. In most disputed cases, the agency must decide whether a neurosis, such as depression or anxiety, is so severe that it renders an individual unable to work, or that a chronic soft tissue condition, such as back pain, is so severe that it renders an individual unable to work. Finally, while it is certainly true that most AFDC beneficiaries have limited educations that impair their ability to express themselves effectively in writing, most also lack the skill needed to engage in effective cross-examination of opposing witnesses in the oral hearings the Court required in *Goldberg* or the financial resources that would enable them to hire representatives who possess those skills.

Second, in retrospect, it is easy to identify *Goldberg* as the high water mark in the Court's due process decision-making. *Goldberg* is the only case in which the Court has held that due process requires an agency to make available a pre-deprivation oral evidentiary hearing. Perhaps that is because the Court has not encountered any other context that presented as compelling a case for requiring an agency to provide a pre-deprivation oral evidentiary hearing as did AFDC. There were enough other developments in the six years that separated the Court's opinions in *Goldberg* and *Mathews* to cause many scholars to believe, however, that the difference in the results of the two cases was attributable in part to the results of a rethinking process on the part of some of the Justices who joined both the majority opinion in *Goldberg* and the majority opinion in *Mathews*.

In the wake of the issuance of the Supreme Court's opinion in *Goldberg*, many participants in a wide variety of agency decision-making processes filed actions in which they alleged that they were deprived of property, within the meaning of the far more expansive definition of property the Court adopted in *Goldberg*, and that nothing less than a pre-deprivation oral evidentiary hearing would satisfy due process. Plaintiffs prevailed in lower courts in many of those cases, and many agencies complained that they lacked the resources to comply with the many court opinions that interpreted the Due Process Clause to require them to use decision-making procedures far more expensive and time-consuming than the procedures the agencies had used in the past.

Studies also began to appear that seemed to support the claims of the Justices who dissented in *Goldberg*. The dissenting Justices claimed that the majority had underestimated significantly the cost of the procedures the Court required—the third factor the Court included in the three-part test the Court subsequently announced in *Mathews*. Studies found that the costs of requiring pre-deprivation oral evidentiary hearings in AFDC cases were high. The number of cases in which AFDC beneficiaries demanded oral evidentiary hearings increased significantly once agencies were required to provide pre-deprivation hearings, rather than post-deprivation hearings. A beneficiary has nothing to lose and much to gain by demanding a pre-deprivation oral evidentiary hearing, since an individual who claims to be eligible for AFDC benefits is unlikely to have enough assets or earning power to be subject to a successful recoupment action by the government if she is determined to be ineligible for the benefits. Even if the applicant loses after the hearing, she will have obtained about a year's worth of benefits that she will have spent by the time she loses. The added costs of the pre-deprivation hearing requirement fell into two categories— the cost of hiring large numbers of lawyers to serve as administrative judges to preside in the much larger number of contested cases, and the cost of the unrecoupable benefits that were provided to the large number of individuals who demanded a pre-deprivation oral evidentiary but who were determined to be ineligible after receiving such a hearing.

Moreover, as the dissenting Justices predicted, much of the added cost of the new procedures came out of the pockets of the very class of individuals the Court was attempting to benefit. Legislative bodies are reluctant to increase an agency's appropriated funds to cover the cost of judicially-mandated additional procedures that the legislature considers unnecessary. If a court mandates expensive new procedures a legislature considers unnecessary, and the legislature declines to increase the agency's funding by the amount needed to cover those added costs, the agency has no choice but to reduce its spending for other purposes, e.g., by increasing the stringency with which it applies eligibility criteria, thereby denying benefits to individuals who would have received them in the absence of the judicial decision. The dissenting Justices also predicted accurately that the decision in *Goldberg* would harm welfare recipients by inducing agencies to engage in lengthy investigations of each individual's claim of eligibility before adding an applicant to the welfare roles. After *Goldberg*, agencies that had been quick to add applicants to welfare roles with little investigation of their claims of eligibility because the agencies expected to be able to remove any individual who was determined to ineligible quickly and easily changed their practices once they recognized that they could not quickly and easily correct an error they had made by adding an ineligible individual to the welfare roles.

The many unintended adverse effects of the *Goldberg* decision raised doubts whether the decision actually conferred net benefits on the needy individuals the Court was attempting to benefit. Recognition of those unintended adverse effects by a majority of Justices also contributed to the far more cautious approach the Court took in its post-*Goldberg* due process decisions, beginning with the Court's decision in *Mathews* just six years after it decided *Goldberg*.

The *Goldberg* Court's formulation of the test to determine whether a statutory provision creates "property" for due process purposes also is an implicit invitation to the legislature to amend applicable statutes to preclude courts from requiring agencies to adopt decision-making procedures that the legislature considers unnecessary and unduly expensive. Legislatures sometimes accept that invitation. The *Goldberg* Court held that AFDC benefits were "property" because "they are a matter of statutory entitlement for those eligible to receive them." AFDC benefits qualified as entitlements because the AFDC statute took the form of an entitlement statute, e.g., if you have the following characteristics, you are entitled to receive the following benefits. In 1996, Congress repealed the AFDC statute and replaced AFDC benefits with Temporary Assistance for Needy Families (TANF). Congress took great care to avoid characterizing the temporary benefits made available under TANF as an entitlement. In fact, Congress included the following provision in the statute in which it replaced AFDC with TANF: "NO INDIVIDUAL ENTITLEMENT.—This part shall not be interpreted to entitle any individual . . . to assistance under any State program funded under this part." Replacement of AFDC with TANF is part of an ongoing trend in which both courts and legislatures are gradually reducing both the scope of due process and the nature of the procedures required by due process.[58] Judicial decisions interpreting and applying the Due Process Clause are likely to continue to influence agency choices of decision-making procedures, however.

E. Judicial Review

1. *Procedural Errors*

An agency action that is taken through adjudication can be subjected to judicial review on many grounds. One that is invoked with considerable frequency is alleged procedural error. If a court concludes that an agency used procedures that failed to comply with the Constitution, a statute, or an agency rule that is designed to confer a valuable procedural right, a court will vacate the agency action and remand the proceeding to the agency if the court believes that the procedural error prejudiced the party that is seeking review. Courts apply to procedural errors made by agencies

---

58. For a more detailed discussion of this trend, see Richard Pierce, The Due Process Counterrevolution of the 1990s? 96 Colum. L. Rev. 1973 (1996).

the same version of the harmless error test they apply to district courts.[59] The sources of the procedural requirements that can be the basis for a court decision vacating and remanding an agency action taken in an adjudication are described in sections A through D of this chapter.

2. *Substantial Evidence*

APA § 706(2)(E) instructs a reviewing court to "hold unlawful and set aside agency ... findings ... found to be unsupported by substantial evidence in a case subject to sections 556 and 557 of the title [the sections that describe formal adjudication] or otherwise reviewed on the record of an agency hearing provided by statute ..." In addition, many statutes that authorize agencies to take various actions contain provisions that instruct a court to review agency findings of fact through application of the substantial evidence standard even when the agency does not use formal adjudication. Thus, the substantial evidence standard applies to all findings of fact that are made in formal adjudications and to all findings of fact made in informal adjudications if the findings were made in the process of taking an action that is authorized by a statute that instructs reviewing courts to apply the substantial evidence standard.

The substantial evidence standard is highly deferential to the agency that makes the findings. The Supreme Court described the test in the 1930s:

> 'It means such relevant evidence as a reasonable mind might accept as adequate to support a conclusion' ... and it must be enough to justify, if the trial were to a jury, a refusal to direct a verdict when the conclusion sought to be drawn from it is one of fact for the jury.[60]

The evidence before an agency often can support opposite findings. In that common situation, the reviewing court must uphold either of the inconsistent findings.

During the 1940s, some circuit courts interpreted the test to apply only with reference to the evidence that supports the agency finding. As so interpreted, it would require a court to uphold an agency finding even if the evidence that contradicts the finding is overwhelming, as long as there is enough evidence in support of the

---

59. Shinseki v. Sanders, 556 U.S. 396 (2009).

60. NLRB v. Columbian E. & S. Co., 306 U.S. 292 (1939), quoting from Consolidated Edison Co. v. NLRB, 305 U.S. 197 (1938).

finding to satisfy the test. The Supreme Court clarified the test in 1951, however, by holding that a reviewing court must consider the whole record when it applies the test; the court must "take into account whatever in the record fairly detracts from" the agency finding, as well as the evidence that supports the finding.[61] Thus, a court must uphold an agency finding if a reasonable person could make such a finding after considering both the evidence in support of the finding and the evidence that is inconsistent with the finding.

The deferential substantial evidence test applies to an agency finding, not to the finding of an ALJ. Thus, if the agency makes a finding that is the opposite of the ALJ's finding, a reviewing court must uphold the agency finding if any reasonable person could make such a finding even if a reasonable person could as easily make the finding the ALJ made. The ALJ's opinion, including the ALJ's findings of fact, are considered part of the record for purposes of applying the substantial evidence test to an agency's findings of fact.[62] The reviewing court must apply the deferential substantial evidence test to an agency finding, rather than an inconsistent ALJ finding, even when the finding depends on the veracity of the witnesses who testified before the ALJ, although the court can attach greater significance to the inconsistent finding of an ALJ in cases in which witness veracity is particularly important.[63] Studies have found that courts reject agency findings more frequently when the agency makes findings inconsistent with the findings of the ALJ who presided at the hearing or when a member of a multi-member agency, e.g., an NLRB Commissioner, dissents with respect to a finding made by the majority.[64]

Substantial evidence can consist entirely of hearsay that would be inadmissible in a judicial trial even if the only admissible evidence before the agency is inconsistent with the agency finding if the reviewing court considers the hearsay evidence reliable.[65] The facts of the case in which the Supreme Court announced that rule illustrate its wisdom. In finding that an applicant for disability benefits was not so disabled that he was unable to obtain any job in the U.S. economy—the substantive standard—the Social Security Administration (SSA) relied on the detailed written reports of five specialists, each of whom had performed diagnostic tests on the

61. Universal Camera Corp. v. NLRB, 340 U.S. 474 (1951).

62. Id.

63. FCC v. Allentown Broadcasting Corp., 349 U.S. 358 (1955).

64. Frank Cooper, Administrative Law: The Substantial Evidence Rule, 44 A.B.A.J. 945, 1002 (1958).

65. Richardson v. Perales, 402 U.S. 389 (1971).

applicant and concluded that he was not disabled, rather than on the unsupported live testimony of the applicant's personal physician, a general practitioner who had performed no diagnostic tests. Like other agencies that adjudicate cases through use of formal adjudication, SSA has a rule that authorizes an ALJ to issue a subpoena to require a hearsay declarant to appear at a hearing to be cross-examined if the party who requests the subpoena provides an offer of proof in which it describes its reasons for skepticism with respect to the declarant's written submission and its reasons for believing that it can cast doubt on the accuracy of that submission through cross-examination. The existence of such rules provides additional assurance that an agency will not rely on unreliable hearsay as the basis for a finding of fact.

Courts often combine the deferential substantial evidence test with the duty to engage in reasoned decision-making described in the next section of this chapter. Thus, for instance, a court can reject an agency finding of fact that is based on enough evidence to satisfy the substantial evidence test in an abstract sense if the agency does not explain why it chose to rely on some items of evidence and to discount or disbelieve other items of evidence.[66]

3.   *Arbitrary and Capricious*

APA § 706(2)(A) instructs a reviewing court to "hold unlawful ... agency action ... found to be ... arbitrary, capricious, an abuse of discretion...." The arbitrary and capricious standard applies to all agency actions, including all formal adjudications and all informal adjudications. The standard has different meanings in different contexts, however. In 1935, the Supreme Court upheld an order issued by a state agency and rejected a claim that the agency action was arbitrary and capricious.[67] The Court described the version of the arbitrary and capricious test it applied in the following passage:

> [I]f any state of facts reasonably can be conceived that would sustain [the order], there is a presumption of the existence of that state of facts, and one who assails [that presumption] must carry the burden of showing ... that the action is arbitrary and capricious.

---

66. See, e.g., Vemco v. NLRB, 79 F.3d 526 (6th Cir. 1996) (vacating agency finding because agency did not explain why it credited unsupported testimony of witness with dubious credibility and rejected contrary testimony that was supported by contemporaneous notes); Adorno v. Shalala, 40 F.3d 43 (3d Cir. 1994) (vacating agency finding because it did not explain why it rejected probative evidence).

67. Pacific States Box & Basket Co. v. White, 296 U.S. 176 (1935).

That version of the arbitrary and capricious test is so deferential that it is nearly impossible for a petitioner to win or for an agency to lose when a court applies it to an agency action. It does not require an agency to support its action with any findings, any evidence, or any reasons. Instead, it requires the petitioner to prove that there is no plausible set of facts or reasoning that might support the action. Courts still use this version of the arbitrary and capricious test in some circumstances, e.g., when a petitioner challenges a statute as a violation of the Equal Protection Clause of the Fourteenth Amendment and the statute does not involve a fundamental right, like speech, or a suspect classification, like race.[68] Modern courts no longer apply this version of the test, however, when a federal court is called upon to determine whether an agency action is arbitrary and capricious as that phrase is used in the APA.

Courts apply the arbitrary and capricious test to agency findings of fact in some cases and to agency reasoning in all cases. Since the substantial evidence test applies only to agency findings made in formal adjudications or in adjudications conducted pursuant to statutes that explicitly incorporate the substantial evidence test, most informal adjudications are not subject to the substantial evidence test. Yet, reviewing courts feel the need to apply some test to determine whether a finding made by an agency in an informal adjudication is adequately supported by the available evidence. Courts use the arbitrary and capricious test to review findings of fact made by agencies in informal adjudications. In this context, the meaning of the test is not entirely clear.

The Supreme Court has often said that the arbitrary and capricious test is less demanding and more deferential than the substantial evidence test when the two are applied to agency findings of fact.[69] The Court has never explained the differences between the two tests, however, and many scholars and circuit court judges are skeptical that they actually have different meanings or effects in the context of judicial review of findings of fact. Thus, for instance the Court of Appeals for the D.C. Circuit often refers to the difference between the two tests as "semantic."[70] Of course, the nature of the "evidence" that supports or detracts from an agency finding may differ in an informal adjudication. If the agency has chosen to rely entirely on a written exchange of data and views to adjudicate a dispute, the evidence available to both the

68. See Laurence Tribe, American Constitutional Law §§ 16–1, 16–2 (2d ed. 1988).

69. E.g., Abbott Laboratories v. Gardner, 387 U.S. 136, 143 (1967).

70. E.g., Association of Data Processing Service Organizations v. Board of Governors, 745 F.2d 677 (D.C. Cir. 1984).

agency and the court will consist solely of the written submissions
of the agency and the other parties.

Courts apply the arbitrary and capricious test to agency reasoning in all cases, including all formal and informal adjudications.
In one of its early attempts to explain the arbitrary and capricious
test, the Supreme Court provided an unhelpful and seemingly
inconsistent description: the test is "thorough," "probing," "in-
depth," "searching," and "careful," but "the ultimate standard of
review is a narrow one."[71] The Court provided its most helpful and
most definitive description of the test in its landmark 1983 opinion
in Motor Vehicle Manufacturers Ass'n v. State Farm Mutual Automobile Insurance Co.[72]:

> Normally, an agency rule would be arbitrary and capricious if
> the agency has relied on factors which Congress has not
> intended it to consider, entirely failed to consider an important
> aspect of the problem, offered an explanation for its decision
> that runs counter to the evidence before the agency, or is so
> implausible that it could not be ascribed to a difference in view
> or the product of expertise.

The Court announced that interpretation of the arbitrary and
capricious standard in the context of review of a rule an agency
issued through the use of informal rulemaking. The *State Farm* test
has particular significance in that context, so it will be discussed in
detail in § 4G(2), but it applies as well to agency adjudications. The
State Farm test is often referred to as the duty to engage in
reasoned decision-making. It requires an agency to explain how it
reasoned from the available evidence to its findings and then to its
conclusions. If a court determines that an agency did not adequately explain the reasoning process that led it to take a particular
action, a court can vacate the action and remand the matter to the
agency.

One of the most important components of the duty to engage in
reasoned decision-making is the duty to explain departures from
precedent and/or from previously announced policies. Courts recognize that agencies must have the discretion to change their course
of action based on changed circumstances and/or new understandings of the relationships among phenomena. Thus, for instance,
EPA must have the discretion to redefine a statutory term like
"pollutant" to include gases that contribute to global warming if
EPA concludes that emissions of such gases are harming the
environment by inducing global warming. An agency has the discre-

---

71. Citizens to Preserve Overton   **72.** 463 U.S. 29 (1983).
Park v. Volpe, 401 U.S. 402 (1971).

tion to depart from its precedents and/or from its previously announced policies if, but only if, its new course of action remains
within statutorily described boundaries,[73] is accomplished through
use of legally-permissible decision-making procedures,[74] and is acknowledged and explained by the agency. If an agency acts in a
manner that is an unacknowledged or unexplained departure from
precedent or policy, a court will vacate the agency action as arbitrary and capricious.[75]

It is easy for a court to apply the arbitrary and capricious test
to an action that an agency takes through use of formal adjudication because the agency is required by statute to issue an opinion
that includes findings and conclusions that can be used as the basis
for judicial application of the arbitrary and capricious test.[76] When
an agency acts instead through use of informal adjudication, the
court often has a more difficult task. An agency that uses informal
adjudication may issue an opinion that includes findings and conclusions, but it is not required to do so, and no court can vacate the
agency's action for declining to use procedures that are not required by statute or by the Constitution.[77] In that situation, the
reviewing court can remand the proceeding to the agency to allow
the agency the opportunity to provide the court with an explanation
for its action sufficient to allow the court to apply the arbitrary and
capricious test.[78]

4. *Errors of Law*

APA § 706 instructs reviewing courts to "decide all relevant
questions of law, interpret constitutional and statutory provisions"
and to "hold unlawful and set aside agency action ... found to be
... not in accordance with law." Most of the issues of law addressed by an agency consist of interpretation of provisions of
statutes the agency has been assigned to implement. The methods
used by courts to review that large category of issues are so
important and so complicated that they are discussed separately
and in detail in chapter 5. Sometimes, however, an agency has
occasion to interpret a provision of a statute that the agency has
not been assigned to implement, e.g., the APA or the National

---

73. See chapter V.

74. See sections B and C of chapters
3 and 4.

75. INS v. Yang, 519 U.S. 26, 32
(1996); Atchison, Topeka & S.F.R. v.
Wichita Board of Trade, 412 U.S. 800,
808 (1973).

76. See § 3B.

77. See § 3C.

78. PBGC v. LTV Corp., 496 U.S.
633 (1990).

Environmental Policy Act (NEPA), or to resolve a dispute that requires it to identify and to apply common law principles. In situations of that type, the reviewing court accords no deference to the agency's resolution of the issue and uses a de novo approach in adopting its own independent interpretation of the statute or explication of the common law principle. That approach makes sense because courts have expertise superior to that of agencies in interpreting statutes of general applicability and in identifying and applying common law principles.

5. Record on Review

Agency actions taken through use of adjudication are subject to the "record rule." The Supreme Court has held repeatedly that a court must limit its review of an agency action to "the administrative record already in existence, not some new record made initially in the reviewing court," and that "except in rare circumstances," a court must remand the matter to the agency for further explanation if the court determines that the record is inadequate to permit the court to engage in review.[79] Of course, the nature of the record compiled at the agency will depend on the procedures the agency used. The record of a formal adjudication will look like the record of a trial court proceeding. It will include pleadings, transcript, exhibits, briefs, the Initial Decision of the ALJ, briefs on and opposing exceptions to that Decision, and the agency's final decision. The record of an informal proceeding can consist of a quite different set of materials. If the agency conducted a paper hearing, for instance, the record is likely to include: (1) the public notice or complaint in which the agency initiated the proceeding, explained its purpose, and identified the issues it expected to be disputed; (2) any materials the agency made available to support its view of the relevant facts, applicable law, and policy-based reasoning; (3) any materials submitted by other parties to support their views of the relevant facts, applicable law, and policy-based reasoning; and, (4) the agency's opinion in which it resolves the dispute and sets forth its reasoning in support of its resolution. If the agency has chosen to use an even less formal decision-making procedure, such as a brief statement in which it summarily resolves a dispute based on its consideration of materials submitted by one or more parties, the record on review will consist only of the materials considered by the agency and the agency's brief statement resolving the dispute. In many cases of that type, the reviewing court concludes that the brief statement in which the agency resolves the dispute is inade-

---

79.   E.g., Florida Power & Light Co.
v. Lorion, 470 U.S. 729, 743–44 (1985).

quate to allow the court to apply the arbitrary and capricious test to the agency action. In that situation, the court remands the matter to the agency to allow it to provide an explanation for its action that is sufficient to permit the court to review the action.

The Supreme Court recognizes that there may be "rare circumstances" in which a reviewing court can go beyond the record before the agency in the process of reviewing the agency action. The Supreme Court has not identified those "rare circumstances," but each circuit has identified a relatively narrow set of circumstances that might justify a court decision to go beyond the record compiled by the agency. Thus, for instance, the Ninth Circuit applies four exceptions to the record rule:

> (1) if admission is necessary to determine whether the agency has considered all relevant factors and has explained its decision, (2) if the agency has relied on documents not in the record, (3) when supplementing the record is necessary to explain technical terms or complex subject matter, or (4) when plaintiffs make a showing of agency bad faith.[80]

The Ninth Circuit is willing to depart from the record rule in more circumstances than some other circuits. Thus, for instance, some circuits do not allow a reviewing court to go beyond the record "to determine whether the agency has considered all relevant factors and has explained its decision."

6. *De Novo Review*

De novo review of federal agency actions is exceedingly rare. APA § 706(F) authorizes a court to "hold unlawful and set aside agency action ... found to be ... unwarranted by the facts to the extent that the facts are subject to de novo review by the reviewing court." It is rare, however, for facts found by an agency to be subject to de novo review. De novo review of such facts is allowed only when a statute specifically instructs a court to engage in de novo review of agency findings[81] or when a petitioner presents to the court powerful evidence that the agency has acted in bad faith by claiming to base its decision on legitimate factors when the actual basis for its decision was improper, e.g., a bribe or bias based on race or national origin.[82] Of course, courts sometimes engage in de novo review of agency conclusions of law, but that complicated topic is discussed in detail in chapter 5.

---

80. Lands Council v. Powell, 395 F.3d 1019 (9th Cir. 2005).

81. E.g., 7 U.S.C. § 2022.

82. E.g., Latecoere International v. Department of Navy, 19 F.3d 1342 (11th Cir. 1994).

F. Estoppel, Res Judicata, Collateral Estoppel, and Agency Non–Acquiescence in Judicial Decisions

Many doctrines that apply to adjudications conducted by courts have somewhat different meanings and applicability to agencies and agency adjudications.

1. *Equitable Estoppel*

When someone relies to his detriment on a representation made by an agent for a firm, the firm is estopped from denying the truth of the representation in litigation. Thus, for instance, if an agent of an insurance company erroneously tells a policyholder that his insurance will cover a car he is considering buying, and the policyholder relies on that statement as the basis to buy the car without obtaining insurance from another company, the insurance company cannot deny the truth of the agent's representation if the car is destroyed on the way home from the dealership and the policyholder makes a claim for the loss of the car. In analogous circumstances, the Supreme Court held that the government agency that insures crops was not estopped from denying that a policyholder's crop was covered after the policyholder had planted the crop based on the erroneous representation of an agent for the agency that the crop would be covered.[83]

The Supreme Court has never upheld a lower court opinion that applied equitable estoppel (or its close relative, promissory estoppel) against the government, and it has come close to saying that equitable estoppel is never available against the government. It has stopped barely short of that statement, however, and it has suggested that estoppel *might* be available in the rare case in which a government employee engaged in "affirmative misconduct" through which he misled an individual into acting to his detriment.[84]

There are both formal and policy-based reasons for the Court's extreme reluctance to allow equitable estoppel against the government. The formal reasons are based on the provisions of the Constitution that allocate power exclusively to specified institutions. Thus, for instance, allowing an individual to obtain government benefits to which the individual is not statutorily entitled through application of equitable estoppel would be a violation of the

---

83. FCIC v. Merrill, 332 U.S. 380 (1947).

84. Heckler v. Community Health Services of Crawford County, 467 U.S. 51 (1984).

Appropriations Clause, since no legislation that had its origin in the House of Representatives authorized such a payment of benefits.[85] Such a judicial decision would have the effect of allowing an employee of the executive branch to appropriate funds.

The policy-based reasons are rooted in a desire to avoid discouraging agencies from refusing to provide informal advice out of fear of potential liability for giving erroneous advice. Most agencies provide several means through which regulatees and beneficiaries can obtain advice and guidance relevant to the statutes the agency implements. The means vary from quick, informal means, e.g., the 800 number IRS provides the general public, to formal mechanisms that often require assistance of counsel and often require a year or more to obtain an answer to a question, e.g., a request for an IRS letter ruling. Not surprisingly, the quick, informal means of obtaining agency advice have high error rates. If agencies could be estopped from acting in a manner inconsistent with erroneous informal advice provided by an agency employee, many agencies would respond by abandoning their mechanisms that now provide quick, informal advice. Courts believe that would be a bad result because agency mechanisms that provide quick, informal advice are valuable to the public even if the advice is wrong 10–20 per cent of the time.

2.　*Res Judicata and Collateral Estoppel*

Unless Congress instructs courts to the contrary in the case of a particular agency, res judicata and collateral estoppel apply to a federal agency finding of adjudicative fact to the same extent and in the same manner as to a finding of adjudicative fact by a court, if the agency used adequate procedures in the process of making the finding.[86] Circuit courts differ with respect to the procedures they find adequate for this purpose. Some courts conclude that any procedure that satisfies due process, potentially including a written exchange of data and views, is adequate, while others require a finding made through use of a procedure that resembles a judicial trial or formal agency adjudication in order to give a finding res judicata effect. Res judicata and collateral estoppel are applicable to a state agency finding of adjudicative fact if the courts of the state would give the finding res judicata or collateral estoppel effect.[87]

---

85. Office of Personnel Management v. Richmond, 496 U.S. 414 (1990).

86. Astoria Federal S & L v. Solimino, 501 U.S. 104 (1991).

87. University of Tennessee v. Elliott, 478 U.S. 788 (1986).

Res judicata and collateral estoppel never apply to a finding of legislative fact for good reason—legislative facts sometimes change, and our beliefs with respect to legislative facts frequently change. Thus, for instance, if res judicata and collateral estoppel applied to decisions of thirteenth century courts, all courts would continue to be bound by the finding that the earth is flat, and if they applied to twenty-first century EPA findings, that agency would never be able to revisit its 2006 finding that carbon dioxide is not a pollutant no matter how much evidence it received thereafter to support the widespread belief of scientists that carbon dioxide emissions are a major cause of global warming.

Res judicata applies to a judicial decision against an agency with respect to an issue of law, but collateral estoppel never applies against the government on an issue of law.[88] Thus, for instance, an agency can continue to argue in other courts in support of its position on an issue of law even though its argument has already been rejected by one or more courts. The government must be allowed to take this course of action in order to allow the Supreme Court to wait until several circuit courts have reached independent, and potentially inconsistent, conclusions with respect to an issue of law before the Supreme Court provides a definitive resolution of the issue.

3. *Agency Non–Acquiescence in Circuit Court Decisions*

Agencies often non-acquiesce in a judicial decision, i.e., the agency acts in accordance with the court decision in the case in which the court issued the decision, but acts in accordance with the agency's contrary interpretation of the law in all other cases. Thus, for instance, if IRS believes that a provision of the Tax Code applies to a firm and requires it to pay a tax, and a court concludes that IRS is wrong, IRS will refrain from attempting to collect the tax from the firm that prevailed in the court case but will continue to attempt to collect the tax from all similarly-situated firms.

This practice is controversial, particularly when the agency continues to act in a manner that is inconsistent with a circuit court opinion in cases that arise in that circuit. Some of the legal rules that are relevant to this practice are well-settled. Thus, for instance, an agency must act in accordance with a judicial decision in the case in which the court issued the decision, and an agency must act in accordance with a Supreme Court decision in all cases. Yet, an agency must be free to act in a manner that is inconsistent

88. United States v. Mendoza, 464 U.S. 154 (1984).

with a court decision in a jurisdiction other than the jurisdiction in which the opinion was issued. That follows from the unavailability of collateral estoppel on an issue of law against the government and from the need to allow multiple circuit courts to make independent decisions on issues of law before the Supreme Court addresses the issue.

Thus, no matter how an agency reacts to a circuit court decision that resolves an issue of law in a manner that the agency believes to be incorrect, the law that applies to similarly-situated individuals or firms will differ. In the case the court decided, the applicable law is the interpretation adopted by the court. Yet, in cases that arise in other circuits, the applicable law will be the inconsistent interpretation that the agency believes to be correct unless and until a court in that jurisdiction or the Supreme Court rejects the agency's interpretation of the law. This situation can exist for a decade or more until one of four things happens: (1) the Supreme Court agrees with the first court and disagrees with the agency; (2) the Supreme Court agrees with the agency and disagrees with the first court; (3) so many other circuit courts agree with the first circuit court and disagree with the agency that the agency acquiesces in the consensus of circuit court opinions; or, (4) so many other circuit courts disagree with the first court and agree with the agency that the first court reconsiders and overrules its initial decision.

The controversial question is what law the agency should apply in other cases that arise in the circuit that has resolved the issue of law in a manner the agency considers incorrect. If the agency applies its interpretation, courts in the circuit will reverse the agency in every case that raises that issue if an adversely affected party seeks review of the agency decision, and adversely affected parties will be forced to seek judicial review of every agency decision to obtain access to the legal interpretation the circuit court believes to be correct. Yet, if the agency applies the legal interpretation adopted by the circuit court in cases that arise in that circuit and the legal interpretation the agency believes to be correct in cases that arise in other circuits, the law applicable to each individual and firm will differ depending on the region in which the individual resides or does business.

The Supreme Court has not yet resolved the dispute with respect to the practice of agency non-acquiescence in circuit court decisions in cases that arise in the circuit. A panel of the Ninth Circuit concluded that the practice was unconstitutional in a 1983 opinion,[89] but then-Justice Rehnquist, acting in his capacity as Circuit Justice, stayed the Ninth Circuit's decision in an opinion in which he concluded that the Ninth Circuit's opinion was itself unconstitutional.[90] Congress acted in a manner that rendered the underlying dispute with respect to the legal issue moot, and no court has since addressed the question of the validity of the agency practice of non-acquiescence.

G. Maintaining Consistency

One of the primary goals of any system of adjudication is consistency in decision-making—like cases should be decided in like manner. This goal is often difficult to attain. The Social Security Administration's (SSA) system of adjudicating disability disputes illustrates the problem. The SSA bureaucracy initially relies on a "paper hearing," consisting primarily of examination of doctors' reports, to decide whether an applicant is so disabled that he cannot perform any job available in the U.S. economy—the statutory standard.[91] If an applicant for disability benefits is dissatisfied with the decision of the SSA bureaucracy, he can appeal that decision, in which case he receives an oral evidentiary hearing before an SSA ALJ. This is the point at which inter-decisional inconsistency is introduced. Empirical studies of disability decision-making by SSA ALJs have found that the most important explanatory variable is the identity of the ALJ, i.e., the same applicant is likely to be found to be disabled by some ALJs but not by others.[92] SSA's roughly 1400 ALJs vary significantly in the attitudes they bring to the process of adjudicating the hundreds of thousands of disability cases they decide each year. SSA and academic observers have long viewed this as a serious problem. The problem of inter-decisional inconsistency is even worse in the context of asylum. A 2007 study of 273,000 asylum decisions made by 884 asylum officers and 225 Immigration Judges (IJ) found massive inconsistencies in patterns of decisionmaking.[93] Thus, for instance, Columbian applicants have an 88 percent probability of success if their

---

89. Lopez v. Heckler, 713 F.2d 1432 (9th Cir. 1983).

90. Heckler v. Lopez, 463 U.S. 1328 (1983). See also Samuel Estreicher & Richard Revesz, Nonacquiescence by Federal Agencies, 98 Yale L.J. 679 (1989) (arguing that the practice is lawful and appropriate.)

91. See Mathews v. Eldridge, 424 U.S. 319 (1976), discussed in § IIID2.

92. Jerry Mashaw, Bureaucratic Justice (1983); Jerry Mashaw, et al., Social Security Hearings and Appeals (1978).

93. Jaya Ramji–Nogales, Andrew Schoenholtz & Philip Schrag, Refugee Roulette: Disparities in Asylum Adjudication, 60 Stan. L. Rev. 475(2007).

case is assigned to one IJ and only a 5 per cent probability of success if their case is assigned to another IJ in the same office.

There are three non-controversial ways in which an agency can attempt to further the goal of inter-decisional consistency in adjudicatory decision-making. First, it can subject ALJ decisions to review by a higher authority in much the same manner as the Supreme Court and circuit courts use to maintain a tolerable degree of consistency in district court decision-making. Many agencies are able to maintain a high degree of consistency by reviewing every ALJ decision. SSA cannot use review effectively for this purpose because of the extremely large number of decisions issued by its ALJs, however. SSA has an Appeals Council that has the power to review, and potentially to reverse, an ALJ decision, but the Appeals Council is able to review only a small fraction of ALJ decisions.

Second, an agency can establish and implement a system of precedents, in which ALJs are bound by precedents and are instructed to decide cases that are not squarely controlled by a precedent through the process of analogy and distinction. Again, many agencies use such a quasi-common law decision-making process with good results as measured by reference to the consistency criterion. SSA can not use such a system, however, because of the volume of its decisions. SSA opinions are not readily available in a central location, either physical or electronic. Even if they were, the sheer number of such opinions would render them useless as a body of potential precedents. No ALJ decision serves as binding precedent for any other ALJ.

Finally, an agency can borrow from legislatures the device they use to maintain a tolerable degree of consistency—issuance of general decisional rules that bind ALJs. SSA often issues rules for this purpose. Thus, for instance, SSA issued a rule that requires ALJs to use a central grid that determines whether any job in the U.S. economy can be performed by an individual with a specified disability coupled with a specified level of education and experience, rather than to rely on each ALJ's highly incomplete and highly variable understanding of the characteristics and requirements of each job in the country. The Supreme Court upheld that rule,[94] and it has produced a dramatic improvement in decisional consistency with respect to the issue to which it applies and in the class of cases to which it applies.

SSA cannot use rules to further its consistency goal, however, in the common situation in which it is impossible to state generally-applicable objective criteria that can be used to decide a class of

94. Heckler v. Campbell, 461 U.S. 458 (1983).

disputes or recurrent issues. Thus, for instance, SSA's grid rule does not apply to a high proportion of disabled individuals because SSA has not been able to categorize them in any manner that would be useful in determining whether the individual can perform a job, e.g., an individual who has limited mental capacity and who has both moderate chronic anxiety and moderate chronic back pain. Moreover, the highest proportion of contested disability disputes that are resolved by ALJs involve either chronic pain or chronic neurosis, and there are no reasonably objective criteria that can be used to distinguish between pain or neurosis that is so severe that an individual cannot perform the functions of any job and pain or neurosis that an individual can tolerate and still perform the functions required for some job.

SSA has used the non-controversial methods of attempting to obtain a tolerable degree of consistency in ALJ decision-making with disappointing results. In a high proportion of cases, the identity of the ALJ to whom the case is assigned continues to be the most important determinant of whether the individual is found to be disabled. In the 1970s and 1980s, SSA attempted to implement a more controversial potential solution to the problem. Since each ALJ decides a large number of cases each year (about 400 per average ALJ), and since the cases are assigned randomly to ALJs, statistical analysis can be used to determine whether ALJs are applying the same standards in deciding cases. In this situation, there is less than a one per cent probability that an ALJ whose rate of awarding benefits varies from that of the mean ALJ by more than 10 per cent is applying the same standard as the mean ALJ. Since the mean ALJ awards benefits in fifty per cent of cases, and approximately 50 per cent of ALJs award benefits in less than 40 per cent of cases or more than 60 per cent of cases, it is easy to demonstrate that about half of ALJs are applying decisional standards that differ from the standards applied by the mean ALJ. SSA attempted to improve decisional consistency by urging ALJs to grant benefits in 40 to 60 per cent of cases.

ALJs challenged the SSA attempts to improve the decisional consistency of ALJs as a violation of both Due Process and the decisional independence of ALJs guaranteed by the APA, and district courts agreed with the ALJs.[95] The Second Circuit rejected the arguments of the ALJs and upheld the SSA efforts to improve consistency, however.[96] Moreover, scholars concluded that the SSA

---

95. E.g., Association of Administrative Law Judges v. Heckler, 594 F.Supp. 1132 (D.D.C. 1984).

96. Nash v. Bowen, 869 F.2d 675 (2d Cir. 1989).

efforts furthered the values that underlie the Due Process Clause by increasing the probability that like cases would be resolved in like manner.[97] The Supreme Court never got an opportunity to resolve the dispute with respect to the validity of SSA's attempts to improve decisional consistency because SSA abandoned those attempts. SSA's decision to abandon its efforts to improve decisional consistency among its ALJs probably was motivated by its desire to improve its relationship with the district judges who review SSA decisions. The rate of judicial reversal of SSA decisions increased significantly during the period in which it attempted to improve decisional consistency, apparently due to district judges' strong feelings of animosity toward the SSA efforts to impose some degree of control over the patterns of decisions of its ALJs.

The controversy over SSA's efforts to improve decisional consistency among its ALJs is symptomatic of a broader tension that is likely to manifest itself in many other ways in the future. The judicial model of justice that has traditionally dominated thinking about administrative justice in the U.S. seeks to obtain a moral judgment by an independent judicial mind based on consideration of all arguably relevant factors, including subjective criteria that can not be verified or refuted and that are likely to be viewed differently by different decisionmakers. By contrast, the bureaucratic model of justice that has traditionally dominated thinking about administrative justice in most of the rest of the world values accuracy, efficiency, and consistency in decisonmaking through use of a hierarchical structure in which institutional decisionmakers rely exclusively on verifiable or refutable objective criteria.[98]

Gradually, the bureaucratic model has begun to be accepted and applied in the U.S. legal system. Perhaps the best example of the use of the bureaucratic model in the U.S. legal system is the Sentencing Commission—an agency that has the power to issue rules that govern sentencing by federal district judges. The Sentencing Commission was created as a response to the appalling inconsistencies among federal district judges with respect to the sentences they gave to criminal defendants who committed similar crimes. It has improved decisional consistency substantially in that important area. After numerous district courts held that the Sentencing Commission violated due process and separation of powers,

97. E.g., Richard Pierce, Political Control Versus Impermissible Bias in Agency Decisionmaking, 57 U.Chi. L.Rev. 481 (1990); Jerry Mashaw, How Much of What Quality: A Comment on Conscientious Procedural Design, 65 Corn. L. Rev. 823 (1980); Antonin Scalia, The ALJ Fiasco—A Reprise, 47 U.Chi. L. Rev. 56 (1979).

98. Jerry Mashaw, Bureaucratic Justice (1983).

the Supreme Court rejected those arguments and upheld its validity in 1989.[99] The Court's 2000 opinion in which it held the Sentencing Commission unconstitutional as a violation of the Sixth Amendment right to jury trial[100] suggests, however, that the battle between the proponents of the judicial model of justice and the proponents of the bureaucratic model of justice is far from over. We are certain to see many more disputes that are symptomatic of the inherent tension between the two models of justice.

99. Mistretta v. United States, 488 U.S. 361 (1989).

100. Apprendi v. New Jersey, 530 U.S. 466 (2000).

Chapter Four

RULES AND RULEMAKING

A. Introductory Overview

Rules serve many salutary purposes in the administrative justice system. They confine agency discretion, increase the likelihood that agencies will decide like cases in like manner, and provide notice to beneficiaries and regulatees with respect to the rules that affect their benefits and duties. Moreover, rules often enhance the efficiency of an adjudicatory system and render it more effective by providing a definitive resolution of a recurring issue, thereby eliminating the need to litigate the issue in each case.

Most agencies have the power to adjudicate disputes. Any such agency can announce a generally-applicable "rule" of conduct in the same manner as a common law court—by announcing the rule or principle in the course of adjudicating a dispute. The Supreme Court has repeatedly upheld agency discretion to announce generally-applicable rules of conduct in this traditional manner.[1] Agencies also can announce rules through other means, however. All agencies have the inherent power to issue rules of procedure, interpretative rules, and policy statements. An agency is not required to follow any procedures before it issues a rule that falls in one of those categories.

Many agencies also have the power to issue legislative rules, also known as substantive rules. As the name implies, legislative rules have the same binding effect as statutes. Unless a legislative rule falls within one of several exemptions, an agency cannot issue a legislative rule without following one of two procedures. If an agency is required by statute to issue a rule "on the record after an opportunity for agency hearing," the agency is required to use the procedures described in APA §§ 556 and 557. Those are the same provisions that apply to formal adjudications. As discussed in § 3B, they require an agency to conduct an oral evidentiary hearing before an ALJ. That rulemaking process is called formal rulemaking. Few statutes require agencies to engage in formal rulemaking, and an agency that is required to use formal rulemaking usually abandons its efforts to issue legislative rules because the formal

---

1. NLRB v. Bell Aerospace Co., 416   332 U.S. 194 (1947).
U.S. 267 (1974); SEC v. Chenery Corp.,

rulemaking process is so expensive, burdensome, and time-consuming. If an agency is not required to issue rules "on the record," it can issue a rule by using the three-step procedure described in APA § 553: issuance of a Notice of Proposed Rulemaking (NOPR), receipt and consideration of comments from interested members of the public, and issuance of a final rule that is accompanied by a statement of its basis and purpose. This is referred to as the process of informal rulemaking.

Informal rulemaking once was an efficient means through which an agency could issue a rule in only a year or two. It continues to operate in that manner in the context of the thousands of relatively non-controversial rules that agencies issue every year. Informal rulemaking is no longer a quick and inexpensive means of issuing a rule today, however, when an agency uses it to issue one of the one hundred to two hundred major rules that agencies issue every year. When a proposed rule would require regulatees to incur hundreds of millions or billions of dollars in compliance costs, a rulemaking typically takes five to ten years to complete and requires an agency to devote a high proportion of its staff resources to the process of issuing the rule. In the context of issuance of such a major rule, the NOPR typically is several hundred pages long, interested members of the public typically submit comments that total hundreds of thousands of pages and that include numerous studies with inconsistent findings with respect to the underlying issues, and the typical statement of basis and purpose that accompanies the final rule is five hundred to two thousand pages long. Moreover, at the end of that long and expensive process, there is a thirty to forty per cent chance that a reviewing court will reject the rule and remand the proceeding to the agency for further action.

Several factors have contributed to the transformation of the informal rulemaking process from a quick and efficient process to a long, expensive, and burdensome process. First, the Supreme Court adopted an interpretation of the arbitrary and capricious standard of review in the rulemaking context that has two related effects: (1) it encourages firms that dislike a proposed rule to submit voluminous comments critical of the proposed rule, and (2) it requires the agency to provide detailed responses to each criticism contained in comments in order to minimize the risk that a court will reject the rule as the product of arbitrary and capricious agency action. Second, Congress has required many agencies to add expensive and time-consuming procedural steps to the three-step informal rulemaking process. Third, the President has also added procedures that agencies must use when they issue major rules.

The long, expensive, and burdensome nature of the modern informal rulemaking process has changed agencies' incentives. Agencies now minimize their use of the informal rulemaking process to issue legislative rules and attempt where possible to substitute other types of regulatory instruments that can be issued without using the informal rulemaking process. Agencies use interpretative rules, policy statements, and even statements of position taken in enforcement actions in lieu of legislative rules to accomplish their regulatory objectives where possible. That common agency practice has produced a lot of litigation in which regulatees argue that an instrument that an agency claims to be exempt from the rulemaking process is actually a legislative rule which is invalid because the agency did not use the informal rulemaking process to issue the rule. A court then has the unenviable task of deciding whether the instrument or document the agency issued is a procedurally-invalid legislative rule or is instead an interpretative rule or policy statement that is valid because it is exempt from the informal rulemaking process.

Interpretative rules and policy statements are exempt from the procedures agencies must use to issue legislative rules. Agencies vary greatly in the terminology they use to describe various types of pronouncements. Thus, for instance some agencies characterize pronouncements as "guidances," "compliance manuals," "advisories," or any of a number of other labels. For legal purposes, however, each document must be placed in one of the categories described in APA § 553–legislative (or substantive) rule, interpretative rule, general statement of policy, or rule of procedure.

B. Legislative Rules

All agencies have inherent power to issue interpretative rules, policy statements, and procedural rules. Only one type of rule can have a legally-binding substantive effect, however—a legislative rule (sometimes referred to as a substantive rule.) An agency can issue one of the other types of rules at any time without using any procedure, but an agency cannot issue a legislative rule without following the procedure described in APA § 553 unless the rule fits within one of the exemptions described in § F of this chapter. Legislative rules have legally-binding effects that render them functionally indistinguishable from a statute. Thus, for instance, a legislative rule can resolve definitively an issue that otherwise would be subject to case-by-case litigation, thereby eliminating a party's statutory right to a hearing with respect to that issue;[2] a

2. United States v. Storer Broadcasting, 351 U.S. 192 (1956).

legislative rule binds the government as long as it is in effect;[3] violation of a legislative rule can subject the government to tort liability;[4] a legislative rule can pre-empt a state law;[5] and, violation of a legislative rule can be the basis for civil penalties or a criminal conviction.[6]

No agency can issue a legislative rule unless Congress has given it that power. Most statutes are explicit in either conferring or not conferring that power, but courts occasionally are required to decide whether an ambiguous statute grants an agency power to issue a legislative rule. In a famous 1973 opinion, the D.C. Circuit held that FTC had the power to issue legislative rules even though FTC had assumed that it lacked that power for over half a century.[7] The court reasoned that an ambiguous statute should be interpreted to confer on an agency the power to legislative rules because such an interpretation of a statute would allow the agency to perform its functions more effectively. The vintage of that decision, the increased tendency of courts to engage in more formal, positivist reasoning, and the dearth of more recent decisions that address the question renders the approach the D.C. Circuit took questionable today. In a well-reasoned 2002 article, Thomas Merrill and Kathryn Watt criticized the D.C. Circuit opinion and argued that Congress invariably includes in an agency-administered statute a provision that authorizes an agency to penalize an entity for violating an agency rule when Congress intends to grant the agency the power to issue legislative rules, and that the absence of such a statutory provision should have induced the D.C. Circuit to conclude that FTC lacked the power to issue legislative rules.[8] (As discussed in the section B(2)(d) of this chapter, Congress later amended the FTC Act to confer on FTC the power to issue legislative rules, albeit through use of a procedure that is so burdensome that FTC rarely attempts to use the power.)

1. *Formal Rulemaking*

APA § 553 governs the process of issuing a legislative rule. Section 553 describes the three-step process that is referred to as

3. United States v. Nixon, 418 U.S. 683 (1974).

4. E.g., Hines v. United States, 60 F.3d 1442 (9th Cir. 1995).

5. City of New York v. FCC, 486 U.S. 57 (1988).

6. E.g., Touby v. United States, 500 U.S. 160 (1991).

7. National Petroleum Refiners Ass'n v. FTC, 482 F.2d 672 (D.C. Cir. 1973), cert. denied, 415 U.S. 951 (1974).

8. Thomas Merrill & Kathryn Watt, Agency Rules with the Force of Law: The Original Convention, 116 Harv. L. Rev. 467 (2002).

informal rulemaking and that is discussed in detail in the next section of this chapter—issuance of a NOPR, receipt and consideration of comments, and issuance of the final rule with its statement of basis and purpose. Section 553(c) provides, however: "When rules are required by statute to be on the record after opportunity for agency hearing, sections 556 and 557 of this Title apply instead of this subsection." Sections 556 and 557 are the sections that describe the process of formal adjudication discussed in section 3B of this book. It consists of an oral evidentiary hearing presided over by an ALJ.

Until 1972, many courts interpreted the APA to require an agency to use formal rulemaking if the agency was required to conduct a "hearing" before it issued a rule or if the agency was required to create a record of some kind when it issued a rule. The Supreme Court ended that practice with a pair of opinions in which it held that "hearing" is ambiguous and that the statutory requirement of a hearing can be satisfied by use of the notice and comment procedure in the context of a rulemaking.[9] Formal rulemaking is so cumbersome and time-consuming that an agency that is required to use it to issue legislative rules usually gives up its efforts to issue legislative rules. The infamous peanut butter rulemaking illustrates the effects of formal rulemaking. FDA required nine years to use formal rulemaking to decide whether a product must contain 90% or 87.5% peanut products to be called peanut butter.[10] Lobbyists and legislators are well aware of the effects of formal rulemaking, so Congress includes an "on the record" rulemaking requirement in a statute only if it has decided to cripple an agency's efforts to implement the statute.

2. Informal Rulemaking

Unless an agency is required by statute to issue rules "on the record after agency hearing," it can issue a rule by using the three-step process described in APA § 553—issuance of a Notice of Proposed Rulemaking (NOPR), receipt and consideration of comments from interested members of the public, and issuance of a final rule accompanied by a statement of its basis and purpose. As it was originally conceived and implemented, the informal rulemaking process provided an efficient, relatively expeditious, and inexpensive way of issuing a rule. Courts and commentators were

9. United States v. Florida East Coast Ry., 410 U.S. 224 (1973); United States v. Allegheny–Ludlum Steel Corp., 406 U.S. 742 (1972).

10. See Corn Products Co. v. FDA, 427 F.2d 511 (3d Cir. 1970).

virtually unanimous in describing it as vastly superior to the common law method of "rulemaking," in which a court or agency announces a generally-applicable rule of conduct in the process of adjudicating a particular dispute.

a.   Advantages of Informal Rulemaking

The major comparative advantages of the informal rulemaking process lie in four areas—better quality of resulting rules, greater fairness, enhanced efficiency, and greater political accountability. Rules issued through informal rulemaking are systematically superior in quality to rules announced through the process of adjudication for three reasons. First, they are the product of a decision-making process in which all interested members of the public participate, rather than only the parties to a particular dispute. Second, they are issued through a procedure in which the agency considers the effects of alternative rules in the typically wide range of situations in which a rule will affect conduct, rather than only the potentially idiosyncratic facts of a particular dispute. Third, the agency adopts a rule in an informal rulemaking based on its consideration of the instrumental effects of the rule in shaping future conduct, rather than based on the agency's view of the result it considers to be fair in resolving a dispute with respect to the particular past behavior of a party.

Adopting rules through informal rulemaking is systematically fairer than adopting rules through adjudication for three reasons. First, all parties who are potentially affected by a proposed rule, rather than only the parties to a particular dispute, have the opportunity to participate in the process that produces the rule. Second, rules adopted through informal rulemaking provide better notice of the conduct they prohibit or permit because they are invariably more clear and explicit in their content and scope than rules adopted through adjudication. Third, rules adopted through use of informal rulemaking apply to every similarly-situated individual or firm simultaneously, while a rule adopted in the course of adjudicating a dispute involving the conduct of one firm or individual may not be applied to other firms or individuals until the agency adjudicates a dispute involving that firm or individual, potentially years later.

Adopting rules through informal rulemaking is systematically more efficient and effective than adopting rules through adjudication for three reasons. First, by adopting a legally-binding rule that resolves a recurring issue, an agency can avoid the time and expense of relitigating the issue in every case. Thus, for instance, when SSA issued a rule in which it related each job in the economy to particular characteristics of applicants for disability benefits, it eliminated the need to determine whether there is a job that an individual with a specified combination of abilities and disabilities can perform in tens of thousands of cases.[11] Second, because the scope and requirements imposed by a rule are much clearer and more transparent when a rule is issued through informal rulemaking than when a rule is announced in the course of adjudicating a case, rules issued through informal rulemaking are more effective and easier to enforce. Third, because rules issued through informal rulemaking have the same legally binding effect as a statute, they are far more effective because violation of the rule can result in imposition of civil or criminal penalties.

Finally, use of informal rulemaking enhances political accountability by providing an opportunity for elected officials to play significant roles in the rulemaking process. An agency must begin the process of informal rulemaking by issuing a NOPR in which it describes the rule it proposes to issue. The NOPR allows the President and members of the House and Senate to know an agency's plans in time to influence those plans. They can do so either through submission of comments or through the process of "jawboning"—meeting informally with agency officials in an effort to persuade them to adopt the proposed rule, to adopt an alternative to the proposed rule, or to abandon their plan to adopt a rule. Some people criticize informal attempts by politicians to influence the outcome of a rulemaking as illegal and inappropriate. The D.C. Circuit provided a definitive and persuasive answer to those complaints in a particularly well-reasoned 1981 opinion.[12] The Court not only held that elected officials can influence the outcome of rulemakings, it explained why agency receptivity to the urgings of elected officials in policymaking is essential in a democracy:

> Under our system of government, the very legitimacy of general policymaking performed by unelected administrators depends in no small part upon the openness, accessibility, and amenability of these officials to the needs and ideas of the public from whom their ultimate authority derives, and upon whom their commands must fall.

* * *

11. The Court upheld that rule in Heckler v. Campbell, 461 U.S. 458 (1983).

12. Sierra Club v. Costle, 657 F.2d 298, 400–410 (D.C. Cir. 1981). See also

Paul Verkuil, Jawboning Administrative Agencies: Ex Parte Contacts by the White House, 80 Colum. L. Rev. 943 (1980).

The court recognizes the basic need of the President and his White House staff to monitor the consistency of executive agency regulations with Administration policy.

* * *

The authority of the President to control and supervise executive policymaking is derived from the Constitution; the desirability of such control is demonstrable form the practical realities of administrative rulemaking.

* * *

Americans rightly expect their elected representatives to voice their grievances and preferences concerning the administration of our laws. We believe it is entirely appropriate for Congressional representatives vigorously to represent the interests of their constituents before administrative agencies engaged in informal, general rulemaking. . . .

Virtually all judges and Justices recognize the enormous advantages of informal rulemaking. During the 1960s, two Justices felt so strongly about the advantages of the informal rulemaking process that they attempted to persuade a majority of their colleagues to require agencies to use that process, rather than the adjudicatory process, to announce all generally-applicable rules.[13] For reasons that will be discussed in § B6 of this chapter, they were not successful in those efforts. Over the last several decades, the informal rulemaking process has changed significantly in ways that have created so many disadvantages to use of the process that many agencies avoid it whenever possible. The changes have come from four sources, each of which will be discussed in subsequent sections of this book—judicial decisions that have adopted expansive definitions of the notice and statement of basis and purpose requirements of APA § 553,[14] congressional decisions to add other mandatory procedures to the three-step process described in that section,[15] presidential decisions to require agencies to add procedures when they engage in major rulemakings,[16] and a judicial decision that allows agency rules adopted through use of informal rulemaking to have prospective effect only.[17] The expensive, burdensome, and time-consuming process of informal rulemaking applies equally to amendments and rescissions of rules, so obsolete

13. E.g., NLRB v. Wyman–Gordon Co., 394 U.S. 759, 777–778 (1969) (dissenting opinions of Justices Harlan and Douglas).

14. See § 4B(2)(b)–(c).

15. See § 4B(2)(d).

16. See § 4B(2)(e).

17. See § 4B(7).

rules typically remain in effect and unamended for many years after they have become obsolete.

b. Judicial Interpretations of Notice

The NOPR required by APA § 553 must include:

(1) a statement of the time, place and nature of public rule-making proceedings;

(2) reference to the legal authority under which the rule is proposed; and

(3) either the terms and substance of the proposed rule or a description of the subjects and issues involved.

Until the 1970s, agencies and courts took the statutory description of the required contents of a NOPR seriously. Courts routinely upheld NOPRs that consisted of only a page or two of general description of the statutory authority for a rule, its purpose, and its content. Thus a typical NOPR would say something like: "Based on the authority contained in sections 4 and 5 of the Natural Gas Act and in order to further the statutory purpose of protecting consumers from unjust and unreasonable rates, the agency hereby proposes to issue a rule that requires owners and operators of natural gas pipelines to provide third party sellers of natural gas equal access to their facilities and to refrain from discriminating in favor of their production or marketing affiliates." Beginning in the 1970s, courts ratcheted up the NOPR requirements to the point at which they now bear no resemblance to the statutory requirement. To have a decent chance of surviving judicial review today, a NOPR in a major rulemaking must be hundreds of pages long.

NOPRs are regularly challenged as inadequate today through application of one or both of two doctrines that first surfaced in the 70s. The first is often called the logical outgrowth test.[18] It instructs a court to reject a NOPR as inadequate unless the final rule the agency issued is the "logical outgrowth" of the decision-making process that begins with issuance of NOPR and extends through receipt and consideration of comments to the issuance of the final rule. The same doctrine is also referred to as the adequately foreshadowed test. Under that name, the doctrine instructs a court to reject a NOPR as inadequate unless it "adequately foreshadowed" the final rule the agency issued. The adequately foreshadowed version of the doctrine makes more sense than the logical

---

18. One of the first cases to announce and apply the doctrine was Wag- ner Electric Corp. v. Volpe, 466 F.2d 1013 (3d Cir. 1972).

outgrowth version. Given the high potential for an agency to change its mind as a result of receipt of comments, a final rule can be a logical outgrowth of the notice and comment process even if it bears no relationship to anything the agency even hinted it might do in the NOPR. By contrast, the adequately foreshadowed version of the doctrine focuses attention on the function of the NOPR identified in the legislative history of the APA—"to fairly apprise interested persons of the issues involved, so that they can present relevant data or argument."[19]

Courts use logical outgrowth and adequately foreshadowed as functional synonyms. Under either name, the test is difficult to apply in many cases. A final rule almost always diverges from the proposal described in a NOPR, often in significant ways, for good reasons. Agencies often change their minds as a result of receipt and consideration of comments, and agencies often change their minds during the typical multi-year period between the issuance of the NOPR and the issuance of the final rule for a variety of reasons unrelated to the comments the agency received—the agency's understanding of the underlying problem and of its potential solutions may have changed because of general changes in the state of understanding of the issues and/or the agency may have changed its attitude because its leadership has changed and/or the public has elected a new President with a different regulatory philosophy from his predecessor. In each case, a court has the often difficult task of deciding whether the final rule diverges so much from any version suggested in the NOPR that the petitioner was deprived of the opportunity to submit meaningful comments on the version of the rule that the agency adopted. An agency lawyer assigned to draft a NOPR in a major rulemaking has the even more difficult task of predicting each of the many ways in which the agency's thinking might change over the years in which the rulemaking is pending before the agency and referring in some way to each of the many potential alternative versions of the rule the agency might adopt as a final rule.[20]

The second doctrine that modern courts apply is often referred to as the expanded notice doctrine. It had its origin in a 1973 case in which EPA relied on an unpublished study as the primary basis for issuing a burdensome rule.[21] A petitioner that was adversely affected by the rule argued that the agency's NOPR was inadequate

---

19. Sen. Doc. No. 248, 79th Cong., 2d Sess. 200, 258 (1946).

20. For helpful suggestions on how to accomplish that task, see Phillip Kannan, The Logical Outgrowth Doctrine in Rulemaking, 48 Admin. L. Rev. 213 (1996).

21. Portland Cement Ass'n v. Ruckelshaus, 486 F.2d 375 (D.C. Cir. 1973).

because the petitioner had no way of knowing of the existence of the study, much less of the agency's intent to rely on the study. The petitioner made an offer of proof to the reviewing court that convinced the court that the petitioner would have been able to demonstrate the existence of numerous flaws in the study if the petitioner had been given notice of the study before it submitted its comments. The court vacated the rule in an opinion in which it stated a broad proposition: "It is not consonant with the purposes of a rule-making proceeding to promulgate rules on the basis of . . . data that, [to a] critical degree, is known only to the agency." To avoid reversal based on application of that principle, an agency must provide notice of any studies or other data sources on which the agency intends to rely in time for parties to submit comments on those studies.

The expanded notice doctrine creates serious problems in its potential application to a major rulemaking. An agency may rely on scores, or even hundreds, of studies and other data sources to support a major rule. At the time an agency issues a NOPR, it is impossible for it to anticipate all of the sources on which it may rely years later when it issues its final rule. Courts have responded to the practical problems created by the expanded notice doctrine by qualifying it in a variety of ways. Thus, for instance, an agency can rely on newly-available studies if they are not the sole basis for the agency decision and the petitioner can not show that it was prejudiced by its inability to comment on the study.[22]

The logical outgrowth and expanded notice doctrines are based on a defensible method of statutory interpretation. The courts reason that the opportunity to submit comments provided for in APA § 553 can not be effective unless interested parties are given an opportunity to comment on the rule the agency actually issues and the studies the agency actually uses to support that rule. The two doctrines have produced NOPRs that bear no resemblance to the description in § 553, however, and have contributed to the transformation of informal rulemaking from an inexpensive and efficient procedure into an extremely long and expensive procedure.

c. Judicial Interpretations of Statement of Basis and Purpose

APA § 553 requires an agency to "incorporate in the rules adopted a concise general statement of their basis and purpose."

---

22. E.g., Kern Cty. Farm Bureau v. Allen, 450 F.3d 1072 (9th Cir. 2006); Personal Watercraft Industry Ass'n v. Department of Commerce, 48 F.3d 540 (D.C. Cir. 1995).

Until the 1970s, agencies and courts acted in accordance with that statutory requirement. Agencies regularly accompanied the final rules they issued with a statement a few pages long in which the agency provided a general description of the basis and purpose of a rule, and courts regularly upheld such statements as adequate to satisfy the APA. Beginning in the 1970s, however, circuit courts began to require agencies to include in their statements of basis and purpose detailed discussions of their reasons for choosing to act on the basis of the findings of one set of studies rather than studies with inconsistent findings, their reasons for rejecting arguments made in comments, their reasons for choosing one set of rules rather than alternative rules, and the reasoning process they used to proceed from the relevant statutory language and available data to the rules they chose to issue. That, in turn, induced parties who are potentially affected by agency rules to submit lengthy comments that include multiple studies with findings inconsistent with the predicates for the rules proposed by the agency.

As a result of these judicial decisions, no agency would have any chance of eliciting favorable action from a reviewing court if it were to take literally the APA requirement that it include with a final rule a "concise general" statement of its basis and purpose. To have any chance of favorable action by a reviewing court, the statement of basis and purpose that accompanies a major rule must be hundreds or even thousands of pages long; it must be comprehensive and detailed, rather than concise and general. The court opinions that have changed the meaning of the statutory requirement for a statement of basis and purpose are the largest single source of the transformation of informal rulemaking from an efficient inexpensive procedure to a lengthy expensive procedure. Since courts relied on the arbitrary and capricious standard of judicial review as the basis for these decisions, they will be discussed in detail in § G(2) of this chapter.

d. Procedures Added by Congress

APA § 553 requires an agency to use only a three-step procedure to issue a rule, but Congress often adds more mandatory procedures to the informal rulemaking process in the statutes that authorize agencies to issue legislative rules. These additional procedures can take many forms. The most extreme in its effects is contained in the FTC Improvement Act, the Toxic Substances Control Act, and the Consumer Product Safety Act. Each of those statutes requires the agency to allow oral evidence and cross-examination on a "disputed issue of material fact" to the extent the agency "determines to be appropriate and to be required for a full and true disclosure with respect to such issues." Since agencies can not predict when a reviewing court will decide that the agency did not allow enough cross-examination on an issue, agencies that are subject to this open-ended requirement typically allow wide-ranging presentation of oral evidence and cross-examination. The result is a procedure that is functionally indistinguishable from formal rule-making, with the same ultimate results—the agency abandons its efforts to issue legislative rules.

Most of the procedures that Congress requires agencies to add to the rulemaking process do not have such a draconian effect. Thus, for instance, Congress requires EPA and OSHA to create Advisory Committees that must consider and report on an agency's proposed rule before the agency can issue a rule to implement a particular statute. An agency that is subject to such a requirement to use Advisory Committees usually continues to issue some legislative rules, but the Advisory Committee review requirement adds time and cost to the rulemaking process.

e. Procedures Added by Presidents

Each President since Ronald Reagan has required agencies to add more procedures to the rulemaking process when they issue major rules. Through issuance of a series of Executive Orders, Presidents require an agency to calculate the costs and benefits of a proposed major rule, and empower the Office of Management and Budget (OMB) to review each major rule and to require the agency to consider additional information and/or to consult with other government agencies before it issues a major rule. The OMB review and consultation requirement adds some additional uncertain increment to the time and expense of issuing a rule.

3. *Negotiated Rulemaking*

In 1990, Congress enacted the Negotiated Rulemaking Act. The Act was intended to create an alternative consensual process through which an agency could issue a legislative rule without the conflicts, delays, and cost of using the rulemaking process. The statute envisioned a process through which an agency could reach agreement with all of its regulatees and beneficiaries with respect to the terms of a rule to govern some area of conduct. Many agencies have used the negotiated rulemaking process successfully to issue relatively minor or non-controversial rules. The negotiated rulemaking process has not been successful in the context of major controversial rules, however. In that context, empirical research has found that the negotiation process does not save time, money or resources, and that it does not reduce conflict or litigation.[23] Those findings should not come as a surprise. In most cases, it is impossible to identify a set of rules that will satisfy hundreds or thousands of parties with widely divergent interests.

4. Agency Interpretations of Legislative Rules

In its 1945 opinion in Bowles v. Seminole Rock & Sand Co.,[24] the Supreme Court held that an agency's interpretation of its own legislative rule must be upheld unless "it is plainly erroneous or inconsistent with the regulation." That holding has been criticized as inviting agencies to use the informal rulemaking process to issue a few broadly-worded legislative rules and then to resolve all important or controversial issues through the process of interpreting the rules,[25] but the Court continues to accord great deference to agency interpretations of ambiguous legislative rules. The Court reaffirmed the *Seminole Rock* holding in its 1997 opinion in Auer v. Robbins[26] and now refers to the doctrine as *Auer* deference. However, in a 2011 concurring opinion, Justice Scalia stated that he might be receptive to an argument that courts should no longer confer deference on agency interpretations of agency rules.[27] He indicated his agreement with the argument John Manning made in a 1996 article that an agency should not be given deference when it interprets a rule that it issued because such deference encourages agencies to maximize the ambiguity in the rules they issue.[28]

Courts have created two important exceptions to the *Auer* doctrine, however. First, an agency can not apply its preferred interpretation of a legislative rule as the basis to impose a penalty on a firm unless the agency has given the firm prior notice of the agency's interpretation.[29] That exception to *Auer* deference is based on the judicial belief that it would be unfair to impose a penalty on a firm for engaging in conduct that it had no way of knowing was illegal at the time the firm engaged in the conduct. Second, a court

---

23. Cary Coglianese, Assessing Consensus: The Promise and Performance of Negotiated Rule–Making, 66 Duke L.J. 1255 (1997).

24. 325 U.S. 410 (1945).

25. See John Manning, Constitutional Structure and Judicial Deference to Agency Interpretations of Agency Rules, 96 Colum. L. Rev. 612 (1996).

26. 519 U.S. 452 (1997).

27. Talk America v. Michigan Bell Tel. Co., __ U.S. __, 131 S.Ct. 2254 (2011).

28. John Manning, Constitutional Structure and Judicial Deference to Agency Interpretations of Agency Rules, 96 Colum. L. Rev. 612 (1996).

29. E.g., General Electric Co. v. EPA, 53 F.3d 1324 (D.C. Cir. 1995).

will not defer to an agency's interpretation of a legislative rule if the rule merely parrots the language of a statute.[30] That exception to *Auer* deference is based on the judicial belief that agencies should not be encouraged to circumvent the informal rulemaking process by issuing legislative rules that do nothing but parrot statutory language and then using the interpretive process to resolve all important disputes.

5. *Petitions for Rulemaking*

APA § 553(e) requires each agency to provide a right to petition to issue, amend, or repeal a rule.[31] Each agency has rules that govern the petitioning process. The Supreme Court has relied in part on the right to petition as the basis for two important related decisions. First, the Court has held that agency decisions not to begin a rulemaking proceeding in response to a petition for rulemaking are reviewable, albeit through application of a particularly deferential version of the arbitrary and capricious test.[32] Thus, a decision not to begin a rulemaking in response to a petition is an exception to the general presumption that agency inaction is unreviewable discussed in § 7C of this book. Second, the Court has held that a court can not consider an argument that a rule has become obsolete unless and until the party who wants to make that argument to a court first makes it to the agency in a petition for rulemaking that the agency denies.[33]

6. *Mandatory Rulemaking*

During the 1960s and early 1970s, Justices Harlan and Douglas tried to convince their colleagues to require agencies to use the rulemaking process, rather than the process of announcing general principles in individual adjudicatory proceedings, as their exclusive means of announcing rules of general applicability.[34] They believed that the advantages of the informal rulemaking process described in § 4B(2)(a) were so great that agencies should be required to use that process rather than the common law decision-making process through which courts announce rules. During the period 1969–1974, some lower courts believed that the Supreme Court had

---

30. Gonzales v. Oregon, 546 U.S. 243 (2006).

31. 5 U.S.C. § 553(e).

32. Massachusetts v. EPA, 549 U.S. 497 (2007).

33. Auer v. Robbins, 519 U.S. 452 (1997).

34. See, e.g., NLRB v. Wyman–Gordon Co., 394 U.S. 759, 777–778 (1969) (dissenting opinion of Justices Harlan and Douglas).

embraced the position espoused by Justices Harlan and Douglas. That belief was created by a 1969 case that was difficult to interpret because of the confusing language in one of the three opinions[35] and by a 1974 opinion in which the unanimous Court referred to the Harlan/Douglas view with apparent approval in dicta.[36] It quickly became apparent, however, that the Court had not accepted the Harlan/Douglas view. In 1947, the Court clearly held that agencies have discretion to use either case-by-case adjudication or informal rulemaking to announce rules of general applicability,[37] and the Court unequivocally reaffirmed that opinion in a 1974 opinion that it issued after the two poorly-worded opinions that had led some lower courts to believe that the Court had adopted the Harlan/Douglas view.[38]

Despite the nearly unanimous belief of scholars, judges, and Justices that the informal rulemaking process is vastly superior to the common law process of making rules, the Supreme Court gave excellent reasons for rejecting the effort to require agencies to rely exclusively in the informal rulemaking process:

> The function of filling in the interstices of the Act should be performed, as much as possible, through this [informal rulemaking] quasi-legislative promulgation of rules to be applied in the future. But any rigid requirement to that effect would make the administrative process inflexible and incapable of dealing with many of the specialized problems which arise. Not every principle essential to the effective administration of a statute can or should be cast immediately into the mold of a general rule. Some principles must await their own development, while others must be adjusted to meet particular, unforeseeable situations....

Thus, courts cannot compel agencies to use informal rulemaking, and agencies retain discretion to use the common law decision-making process to announce general rules of conduct unless Congress eliminates that discretion in the context of a particular statute or provision of a statute. An agency often has an incentive to use informal rulemaking because of the many advantages described in § 4B(2)(a), but those advantages are offset by the time

---

35. NLRB v. Wyman–Gordon Co., 394 U.S. 759 (1969) (plurality criticizes agency for not using informal rulemaking but upholds rule agency announced in the course of resolving an adjudicatory dispute).

36. Morton v. Ruiz, 415 U.S. 199, 231 (1974) (opinion refers to agency's

failure to use informal rulemaking process as one of numerous reasons for holding the rule invalid).

37. SEC v. Chenery Corp., 332 U.S. 194 (1947).

38. NLRB v. Bell Aerospace Co., 416 U.S. 267 (1974).

and expense of the informal rulemaking process and the inability to issue a rule with retroactive effect through use of that process, as discussed in the next section of this chapter.

Congress sometimes instructs agencies to use the informal rulemaking process to issue rules to implement a statute or a provision of a statute. Thus, for instance, the Medicare and Medicaid Acts and the ambient air standards section of the Clean Air Act can only be implemented through issuance of legislative rules through use of the informal rulemaking process. The only issue that arises in such a situation is the extent to which the agency must resolve important issues in its legislative rules versus the extent to which it can rely on the process of issuing interpretative rules that interpret broadly-worded legislative rules to resolve important issues. That question produced a five-to-four division of the Justices in 1995.[39] All of the Justices agreed that the question necessarily is one of degree—an agency should not be allowed to issue legislative rules so broad that they leave most important issues to be resolved in the interpretative process, but no agency can be expected to resolve all important issues in the legislative rules it issues.

7. *Retroactive Rules*

Until 1988, agencies often issued rules that had retroactive effects, and courts upheld those rules if they satisfied a fairness test. In many situations, the ability to issue a rule with retroactive effect is essential to allow an agency to perform its statutory mission. Thus, for instance, if a regulatory or tax agency proposes to change a rule in a way that is likely to make future transactions more profitable, it must make the final rule retroactive to avoid distorting the incentives of regulatees or taxpayers by inadvertently encouraging them to delay their transactions for the years required to issue the final rule. In 1988, however, the Supreme Court held that an agency can not issue a rule with retroactive effect unless Congress has explicitly granted it the power to issue rules with retroactive effects.[40] Since Congress rarely addresses the retroactivity issue in any way, the effect of the Court's opinion was to preclude virtually all agencies from using the informal rulemaking process to issue rules with retroactive effects. The Court's opinion has also had the unfortunate effect of discouraging agencies from using the informal rulemaking process, since an agency can issue a

---

39. Shalala v. Guernsey Memorial Hospital, 514 U.S. 87 (1995).

40. Bowen v. Georgetown University Hospital, 488 U.S. 204 (1988).

rule with retroactive effect either through the common law decision-making process or by issuing an interpretative rule.

C. Interpretative Rules

Interpretative rules are exempt from the informal rulemaking
process. Agencies issue at least ten times as many interpretative
rules as legislative rules, for a good reason. An agency can issue,
amend, or rescind an interpretative rule at any time without using
any prescribed procedure. By contrast, the process of issuing,
amending, or rescinding a legislative rule is expensive, burdensome,
and time-consuming. If an agency makes a mistake in issuing a
legislative rule, or if a legislative rule becomes obsolete, the agency
cannot amend or rescind the rule without devoting many years and
many thousands of staff hours to the process. Since both agency
errors in issuing rules and obsolescent rules due to changed circumstances are inevitable, an agency takes a high risk of making a
costly, long-lived error if it issues a detailed and highly particularized legislative rule. By contrast, if an agency issues a broadly-
worded, ambiguous legislative rule and then relies primarily on
interpretative rules to particularize the meaning of the legislative
rule, the agency reduces its risk of issuing a legislative rule that it
regrets having issued but cannot easily change. The agency also
gives itself the flexibility to issue interpretative rules that are
mistaken or that become obsolete but that can be amended, replaced or rescinded quickly and at a low cost.

Because of the large differences in the ease and cost of issuing
legislative and interpretative rules, many agencies attempt to minimize their use of legislative rules and to maximize there use of
interpretative rules. A regulatee who is adversely affected by a rule
that an agency claims to be interpretative typically responds by
challenging the rule on the basis that it is actually a legislative rule
and that it is procedurally invalid because the agency did not use
the informal rulemaking process required to issue a legislative rule.
As a result of this recurrent pattern of interaction between agencies
and regulatees, there are a large number of cases each year in
which courts have to decide whether a rule is a procedurally valid
interpretative rule or a procedurally invalid legislative rule.

The process of distinguishing between a legislative rule and an
interpretive rule is often difficult. An interpretative rule is not
legally binding, but courts defer to agency interpretations of statutes and legislative rules,[41] so an interpretative rule often can have
significant effects. A legislative rule can create, change, or eliminate

---

41. See chapter five and § B(4) of
this chapter.

rights and duties. By contrast, an interpretative rule can only clarify or particularize rights and duties created by the statutes and/or legislative rules that the interpretative rule interprets. That distinction can be subtle in some cases, however.

By far the best test for distinguishing between a legislative rule and an interpretative rule was announced and applied by the D.C. Circuit in 1993.[42] The court concluded that a rule is legislative if (1) the agency says that it is legislative; (2) the rule amends a pre-existing legislative rule; (3) the agency would not be able to initiate an enforcement action in the absence of the rule; or, (4) the agency publishes the rule in the Code of Federal Regulations (CFR). The court then applied its four-part test to the rule at issue and held that it was a valid interpretative rule.

The rule at issue in the 1993 case illustrates well the merits and operation of the announced test. The Mine Safety & Health Act authorizes the Mine Safety & Health Administration (MSHA) to issue rules to require mine owners and operators to make reports relevant to the Act. MSHA used informal rulemaking to issue a rule that required regulatees to report any case in which an employee suffers an occupational illness. That rule clearly was a legislative rule both because the agency invoked its power to issue legislative rules and because MSHA could not have brought an enforcement action against any regulatee for failure to report an occupational illness in the absence of the rule. Regulatees complained, however, that the rule was too vague to allow them to know with confidence when they were required to report a case of lung disease as pneumoconiosis—a disease that can only be caused by working in a mine. MSHA responded by issuing a rule it characterized as an interpretative rule in which it described the nature of the xray readings and the nature of the xray readers that would require a regulatee to report a case of lung disease as an occupational illness. Over time, MSHA became convinced that its first interpretative rule failed to describe all of the circumstances in which a combination of a particular type of xray reader and xray reading suggested the likelihood that an individual was suffering from pneumoconiosis. MSHA changed its interpretative rule two times in an effort to insure that it caught all cases of pneumoconiosis. The petitioner challenged the third of those rules on the theory that it was actually a procedurally invalid legislative rule rather than an interpretative rule.

42. American Mining Congress v. Mine Safety & Health Administration, 995 F.2d 1106 (D.C. Cir. 1993).

The court applied its four-part test to support its holding that the rule was interpretative. First, the agency characterized the rule as interpretative and did not claim that it had any legally-binding effect. Second, the rule did not amend the pre-existing legislative rule in which the agency required regulatees to report cases of occupational illness; it merely clarified and particularized that rule. The rule amended the pre-existing interpretative rule in which the agency had specified a different combination of readers and readings as necessary to demonstrate the existence of an occupational disease, but the court recognized that an interpretative rule can amend a pre-existing interpretative rule. Third, the rule was not essential to allow the agency to bring an enforcement action against a firm for failing to report a case of occupational disease; the pre-existing legislative rule was sufficient to permit the agency to bring such an enforcement action. Fourth, the agency did not publish the rule in the CFR.

The D.C. Circuit has made two changes to the four-part test it announced in 1993. First, it noted in a subsequent case that publication of a rule in CFR is "a mere snippet" of evidence that the rule is legislative.[43] The court eliminated that part of the test once it discovered that agencies often publish some of their most important interpretative rules in CFR to maximize public awareness of those rules. Second, beginning in 1997 the D.C. Circuit issued a series of opinions in which it held that an interpretative rule cannot amend a pre-existing interpretative rule. That line of cases is demonstrably wrong; its underlying reasoning is illogical and inconsistent with numerous Supreme Court opinions,[44] but the D.C. Circuit applies it in some cases at present.

The Supreme Court has added another basis on which a court can at least deprive a putatively legislative rule of most of its force. Ordinarily, a court must accord great deference to an agency's interpretation of a legislative rule.[45] That doctrine allows agencies to adopt the common strategy of using informal rulemaking to issue broad, ambiguous legislative rules, and then to clarify and particularize those broadly-worded rules by issuing many interpretative rules. In its 2006 opinion in Gonzales v. Oregon,[46] the Court announced an "anti-parroting" doctrine: an agency is entitled to no deference to its interpretations of a legislative rule that simply

43. Health Insurance Ass'n of America v. Shalala, 23 F.3d 412 (D.C.Cir. 1994).

44. Richard Pierce, Distinguishing Legislative Rules from Interpretative Rules, 52 Admin. L. Rev. 547 (2000).

45. See § B(4) of this chapter.

46. 546 U.S. 243 (2006).

parrots the language of the statute it is supposed to implement. The anti-parroting doctrine makes sense. It precludes an agency from circumventing the informal rulemaking process completely by issuing legislative rules that merely parrot the statute and then using the interpretive process as its exclusive means of making all decisions. The doctrine is difficult to apply, however. A legislative rule rarely, if ever, literally parrots the relevant statutory language; even the rule at issue in *Gonzales* went beyond the words of the statute to some extent. Conversely, no legislative rule can resolve all important issues; all rules are ambiguous in some respects. It follows that a court must engage in a difficult line-drawing process when it decides whether a rule adds so little to the statutory language that it should be characterized as a rule that parrots.

D. Policy Statements

Like interpretative rules, general statements of policy are exempt from the informal rulemaking process. For that reason, they too are popular with agencies. An agency would much prefer to issue just a few broadly worded legislative rules and then to rely primarily on some combination of interpretative rules and policy statements to flesh out the meaning of the legislative rules and to describe the manner and circumstances in which the agency will apply the rules. Of course, as with rules that agencies characterize as interpretative, when an agency issues a document that it characterizes as a policy statement, and a regulatee is adversely affected by the statement, the regulatee challenges the validity of the putative policy statement in court by arguing that it is actually a legislative rule that is invalid because it was not adopted through use of informal rulemaking. This regular pattern of interaction gives rise to many cases in which courts must decide whether a statement that an agency claims to be an exempt policy statement is instead a procedurally invalid legislative rule.

Until 2000, courts resolved disputes of this type by applying the "legally binding" test. If the agency statement was legally binding, it was a legislative rule that could only be issued through use of the informal rulemaking process. If it was not legally binding, but instead merely announced the manner in which the agency planned to act in various circumstances, it was an exempt policy statement. If the statement itself was ambiguous in its intended effect, a court would uphold it in an opinion in which it cautioned the agency that it could never give the statement legally binding effect and that, if the agency did give the policy statement legally binding effect in some case, the court would reverse the action in which the agency gave the policy statement legally binding effect.[47] The legally binding test worked well. It was easy to apply because a court could simply uphold as a non-binding statement of policy any ambiguous agency pronouncement that an agency claimed to be a policy statement and then ensure that the agency remained true to its word by reversing any agency action in which the agency attempted to rely on the statement as if it were a legislative rule.

Unfortunately, in 2000 the D.C. Circuit replaced the legally binding test with a practically binding test.[48] Through application of that test, a court can conclude that an agency statement is a procedurally invalid legislative rule, rather than a policy statement that is exempt from the informal rulemaking procedure, even if the statement is not legally binding, if the agency as a practical matter adheres to the policies stated in its statement most of the time. Other circuits have rejected the practically binding test for good reasons. It is hard to apply, and it defeats the purpose of a policy statement. As the Fifth Circuit recognized, an agency should adhere to its stated policies most of the time; indeed, an agency that departs from its stated policies without adequate explanation is vulnerable to a judicial conclusion that it has acted in an arbitrary and capricious manner.[49]

Even the legally binding test has unfortunate effects in an important class of cases. No agency has resources sufficient to allow it to act against all technical violations of the statutes and rules it implements. The Supreme Court explicitly recognized that important reality in its landmark decision in Heckler v. Chaney,[50] in which it held that agencies have unreviewable discretion not to take an enforcement action in most cases. It would be helpful to regulatees, beneficiaries, and to the politicians who are ultimately responsible for the performance of an agency to know when it will, and will not, exercise its discretion to bring an enforcement action. An agency cannot issue a policy statement that states its enforcement criteria in a clear manner, however, for fear that a court will hold that, by limiting its discretion, the agency has issued a procedurally invalid legislative rule rather than an exempt policy statement.[51] To protect itself from such a judicial conclusion an agency must state its enforcement criteria in fuzzy ways, using

47. See, e.g., Pacific Gas & Electric Co. v. FPC, 506 F.2d 33 (D.C. Cir. 1974).

48. Appalachian Power v. EPA, 208 F.3d 1015 (D.C. Cir. 2000).

49. Professionals and Patients for Customized Care v. Shalala, 56 F.3d 592 (5th Cir. 1995).

50. 470 U.S. 821 (1985), discussed in § 7C of this book.

51. See, e.g., Community Nutrition Institute v. Young, 818 F.2d 943 (D.C. Cir. 1987) (holding that putative policy statement was procedurally invalid legislative rule because it restricted agency's discretion to take enforcement actions).

language like "ordinarily we will not act when" even when the agency knows that it will never act in the circumstances described in its policy statement. Such judicially-induced inaccurate statements of enforcement policies disserve the public.

E. Procedural Rules

Rules of procedure are also exempt from informal rulemaking procedure. Some rules are clearly procedural, rather than substantive, e.g., a rule specifying the size of the pages of briefs and the deadlines for submitting briefs. Many rules are difficult to characterize, however, so the distinction between legislative rules that can only be issued through use of informal rulemaking and exempt rules of procedure often arises in court cases. Thus, for instance, a court held to be substantive, and thus to be procedurally invalid for failure to use informal rulemaking, a rule in which OSHA stated that any firm that did not adopt a "voluntary" cooperative compliance program would be subject to inspection.[52] By contrast, a court held to be an exempt procedural rule a rule in which the Department of Agriculture announced that it was eliminating one of the ways in which a firm that sells food could obtain approval of its labeling.[53] In resolving disputes about whether agency rules are substantive or procedural, courts use the same reasoning process they use to decide whether rules of law are procedural or substantive for purposes of applying the federalism-based distinction the Court announced in Erie Railroad v. Tompkins.[54]

F. Other Exempt Rules

APA § 553 also contains two other exemptions from the informal rulemaking process. First, a rule is exempt if the agency makes a finding that "good cause" requires it to issue the rule without first using the informal rulemaking process and a court upholds the agency finding of good cause. Courts are reluctant to uphold such good cause findings, however. An agency has little chance of persuading a court to uphold a good cause finding unless the agency can persuade the court that there will be a lot of unnecessary loss of life if the agency is required to wait until it completes the informal rulemaking process. Thus, for instance, in the wake of the 9/11 terrorist attacks on the World Trade Center, a court upheld an FAA finding that it had good cause to issue a rule without first engaging in informal rulemaking where the rule empowered FAA to

52. Chamber of Commerce v. Department of Labor, 174 F.3d 206 (D.C. Cir. 1999).

53. James V. Hurson Associates, Inc. v. Glickman, 229 F.3d 277 (D.C. Cir. 2000).

54. 304 U.S. 64 (1938).

revoke the pilot's license of a foreign national upon receipt of notification by the Department of Homeland Security that the foreign national/pilot posed a danger to national security.[55] Even when an agency makes a finding of good cause that a court upholds, the agency almost always couples its issuance of an interim emergency rule with publication of a NOPR in which the agency proposes to make the interim rule permanent and solicits comments on its proposal. Thus, a judicially upheld finding of good cause rarely eliminates the informal rule making process. Rather, it reverses the sequence by allowing the agency to issue the rule on a temporary emergency basis while the agency engages in informal rulemaking to decide whether to make the rule permanent.

Second, the APA exempts rules involving specified subject matters: "a military or foreign affairs function ... or a matter relating to agency management or personnel or to public property, loans, grants, benefits, or contracts." Some of these subject matter exemptions persist and remain important today. Thus, for instance, in 2003 the First Circuit upheld as an exempt rule concerning military or foreign affairs, a rule in which an agency established a security zone around a naval installation. Other subject matter exemptions have been eroded, however, through two means. First, in some cases Congress has enacted statutes in which it has subjected otherwise exempt categories of rules to informal rulemaking. Second, in other cases, agencies have issued rules in which they have bound themselves to use informal rulemaking even though the rules they issue would otherwise fall within a subject matter exemption. Through those two means, many rules that govern eligibility for benefits or permissible uses of public lands are no longer exempt from the informal rulemaking process.

G. Judicial Review of Rules

As discussed in chapter eight, a rule is reviewable only if it constitutes final agency action, it is ripe for review, and the petitioner has exhausted its administrative remedies. Each of those three doctrines is complicated in its potential application to a rule. Generally, a legislative rule is subject to review, though some are subject to review as soon as they are issued while others are subject to review only when the rule is applied in an enforcement proceeding or a benefit eligibility proceeding. Generally, it is much more difficult to obtain judicial review of an interpretative rule or a policy statement because pronouncements of that type do not have a legally binding effect.

55.   Jifry v. FAA, 370 F.3d 1174 (D.C. Cir. 2004).

1. *Procedural Errors*

A court can vacate a legislative rule because of an agency's failure to comply with any of the procedures described in § B of this chapter, e.g., failure to use the formal or informal rule making process, inadequate notice of a proposed rule, an inadequate statement of the basis and purpose of the rule, or failure to comply with a procedural requirement that Congress made specially applicable to rules of the type at issue. A court cannot vacate a rule because the agency did not comply with a procedure the President applied to rules of the type at issue because the Executive Orders in which Presidents have required agencies to comply with additional procedures in issuing some types of rules specify that they are enforceable only by the President and not by a court.[56] A court can not vacate an interpretative rule, policy statement, procedural rule, or other type of rule that APA § 553 exempts from the informal rulemaking process on procedural grounds because an agency is not required to follow any procedure in the process of issuing such a rule.

2. *Arbitrary and Capricious*

The most frequent basis on which courts reject rules is a judicial conclusion that the rule is arbitrary and capricious. The arbitrary and capricious test has changed dramatically over the years. In 1935, the Supreme Court held that a rule is not arbitrary and capricious "if any state of facts reasonably can be conceived that would sustain it, there is a presumption of the existence of that state of facts, and one who assails the classification must carry the burden of showing by a resort to common knowledge or other matters which may be judicially notice, or to other legitimate proof, that the action is arbitrary...." Under that formulation of the arbitrary and capricious test, an agency needed no evidence, no record, and no statement of reasons to support a rule; rules were rarely challenged; and challenges were rarely successful. That situation changed only slightly with the passage of the APA in 1946. The APA required an agency to include with each legislative rule a "concise general statement of its basis and purpose," so a court had some basis to apply the arbitrary and capricious test to a legislative rule. At least in theory, a court could say that a rule was arbitrary and capricious because the agency's statement of basis and purpose was inadequate. Until 1967, however, a rule rarely could be chal-

---

56. See § 10B(4) for discussion of the Executive Orders.

lenged except in the context of a proceeding to enforce a rule. In that situation, the record a reviewing court used to review the rule was the record of the enforcement proceeding; challenges rarely succeeded even when the agency had provided only a brief statement of the basis and purpose of its rule; and rules were rarely challenged for fear that a violation of a rule followed by an unsuccessful challenge would result in imposition of severe sanctions on the violator.

The environment in which rules were subjected to judicial review changed dramatically in 1967. The Supreme Court announced a new test to determine whether a rule is ripe for review that had the effect of making many rules subject to review as soon as they were issued and before the rule was used as the basis for an enforcement proceeding.[57] After that decision, pre-enforcement challenges to rules became routine, since a regulatee or beneficiary that did not like a rule had everything to gain and nothing to lose by challenging the rule. Courts also changed their attitudes toward the type of statement of basis and purpose an agency needed to provide to avoid a judicial conclusion that the rule is arbitrary and capricious. Since courts that engaged in pre-enforcement review of rules lacked the record of an enforcement proceeding to use as their basis for review, courts began to demand that agencies provide lengthy statements of the basis and purpose of rules so that courts would have an adequate basis to apply the arbitrary and capricious test to rules issued using the informal rulemaking process. Courts admonished agencies not to take seriously the statutory adjectives "concise" and "general" that Congress used in the APA to describe the statement of basis and purpose that must accompany a rule and instructed agencies to tailor their statements of basis and purpose to the realities of the judicial review process.[58]

By 1983, circuit courts were requiring agencies to include in their statements of basis and purpose discussions of all of the agency's sources of data in support of its rule, detailed explanations for its decisions to rely on some data sources rather than others, explanations of its method of reasoning from its beliefs with respect to the underlying facts to its beliefs with respect to the potential beneficial and detrimental effects of its rule, explanations for its belief that its rule was consistent with the language of the statute the agency was implementing, explanations for its decision to choose one rule rather than plausible alternative rules, and responses to any comments critical of its proposed rule submitted by any interested member of the public. If a court concluded that an

57. Abbott Laboratories v. Gardner, 387 U.S. 136 (1967).

58. E.g., Automotive Parts & Ass'n v. Boyd, 407 F.2d 330 (D.C. Cir. 1968).

agency's statement of basis and purpose was inadequate in any respect, the court concluded that the rule was arbitrary and capricious.

This new approach to judicial application of the arbitrary and capricious test to rules adopted through use of informal rulemaking was referred to as the "hard look" doctrine. It gave parties who disliked all or a portion of a proposed rule a powerful incentive to submit voluminous comments critical of the rule, including studies that purported to contradict the agency's beliefs with respect to the patterns of facts that provided the predicates for the rule propose by the agency. The result in a major rulemaking was a statement of basis and purpose several hundred pages long in which the agency discussed hundreds of thousands of pages of comments on the proposed rule. Even when an agency provided such a voluminous statement of basis and purpose, a reviewing court rejected the statement as inadequate and the resulting rule as arbitrary and capricious in about thirty per cent of major rulemakings.

Many observers of the administrative process expected the Supreme Court to issue an opinion in which it rejected the hard look doctrine as inconsistent with both the traditional version of the arbitrary and capricious test and the statutory description of the statement of basis and purpose as concise and general. Instead, however, the Court issued a landmark opinion in which it upheld the hard look doctrine. In Motor Vehicle Manufacturers' Ass'n v. State Farm Mutual Automobile Insurance Co.,[59] the Court stated the arbitrary and capricious test in the following manner:

> Normally, an agency rule would be arbitrary and capricious if the agency has relied on factors which Congress has not intended it to consider, entirely failed to consider an important aspect of the problem, offered an explanation for its decision that runs counter to the evidence before the agency, or is so implausible that it could not be ascribed to a difference in view or the product of expertise.

State Farm involved a challenge to a decision by the National Highway Traffic Safety Administration (NHTSA) to rescind a rule in which the agency had required every auto maker to include in every car marketed in the U.S. after a specified date one of two safety devices—air bags or automatic seat belts. NHTSA supported that rule with studies that purported to show that either device would be equally effective in avoiding a large number of deaths and serious injuries each year and with a prediction that auto makers would respond to the rule by installing air bags or automatic seat

---

59.   463 U.S. 29, 43 (1983).

belts in approximately equal proportions. NHTSA's decision to rescind the rule before it had an effect on new cars was based on its new belief that manufacturers would respond to the rule by installing air bags in only about one per cent of cars and automatic seatbelts in the other ninety-nine per cent and its new prediction that automatic seatbelts would not be effective because they would increase use of seatbelts by no more than five per cent.

No one challenged NHTSA's belief with respect to the way in which auto makers would respond to the rule NHTSA rescinded. By then it was apparent that auto makers would respond primarily by installing automatic seat belts because they are considerably less expensive than air bags. State Farm and other petitioners challenged NHTSA's rescission decision as arbitrary and capricious on two other grounds, however. After first holding that the arbitrary and capricious standard applies in the same manner to rescission and amendment of rules as it does to issuance of rules, the Court agreed with both of the petitioners' arguments.

First, the Court held unanimously that NHTSA's action was arbitrary and capricious because NHTSA did not consider at all the alternative of amending the rule to permit compliance only through installation of air bags—an alternative that would preserve the benefits of the original rule even in the new circumstances in which NHTSA believed that the rule would operate. Second, a five-Justice majority held that NHTSA was arbitrary and capricious because it did not explain adequately why it believed that automatic seat belts would yield only a five per cent increase in use of seat belts when NHTSA had before it two studies that arguably would support a belief that automatic seat belts would produce a much larger increase in use of seat belts. NHTSA had distinguished the studies on the basis that both involved a device called an ignition interlock that would not allow a driver to start a car without first attaching his seat belt and the seat belt of any other front seat passenger. Ignition interlocks were extremely effective in inducing drivers to use seat belts during the year in which NHTSA required them to be installed in new cars, but Congress rescinded the NHTSA rule that required ignition interlocks because the device was unpopular with the driving public. NHTSA pointed out that the ignition interlock was effective largely because it was difficult for most car owners to disconnect and illegal for repair shops to disconnect. By contrast, NHTSA predicted that automatic seat belts would not be effective in inducing drivers to use seat belts because a driver can disconnect an automatic seat belt in about ten seconds. Four dissenting Justices found NHTSA's explanation for its belief that automatic seat belts would be largely ineffective adequate, but a five-Justice majority concluded that it was inadequate.

The *State Farm* test is also referred to as the adequate consideration test. Lower courts regularly apply it as the basis for conclusions that an agency rule is arbitrary and capricious because an agency did not consider "adequately" comments critical of its proposed rule, potential alternatives to that rule, and studies inconsistent with the factual predicates for the rule. Since there are always myriad comments critical of a proposed rule, potential alternatives to the rule, and studies that are inconsistent with the factual predicates for the rule, the *State Farm* test is invariably invoked as one of the arguments petitioners make when they attempt to persuade a court to reject a rule they do not like. Since adequacy is in the eye of the beholder, an agency can not predict the results of judicial application of the *State Farm* test no matter how long and comprehensive the statement of basis and purpose the agency includes with its final rule. Courts regularly reject as inadequate statements of basis and purpose that are hundreds of pages long. The one thing an agency can predict is that the outcome of judicial applications of the test will depend primarily on the political and ideological beliefs of the judges who apply the test. Thus, for instance, Dean Revesz of NYU Law School found that Republican judges rejected as inadequate the reasoning of EPA in support of a rule issued to implement the Clean Air Act in eighty-nine per cent of cases in which regulatees challenged such rules as arbitrary and capricious, while Democratic judges found EPA's reasoning inadequate in only thirteen per cent of such cases.[60]

A court can choose one of two remedies when it concludes that a rule is arbitrary and capricious because the agency did not adequately consider some issue. First, the court can vacate the rule and remand the proceeding to the agency to allow it to decide whether to abandon its attempt to issue the rule, to issue a modified version of the rule that a court might find more palatable, or to reissue the same rule with a new statement of basis and purpose that includes additional discussion of the issue or issues the court determined to have been inadequately considered. Second, a court can remand the proceeding to allow the agency the opportunity to add enough discussion to satisfy the court that the agency adequately considered the issues without vacating the rule. A court often chooses the remand without vacation remedy when the deficiency in reasoning the court detected is relatively minor, the court

60. Richard Revesz, Environmental Regulation, Ideology, and the D.C. Cir- cuit, 83 Va. L. Rev. 1717, 1721 (1997).

believes that the agency is likely to be able to address that deficiency adequately on remand, and vacation would have a disruptive effect.[61] The remand without vacation remedy is controversial, however. Some judges believe that a court lacks the discretion to use it.[62]

As a practical matter, the *State Farm* test has no application to interpretative rules, policy statements, rules of procedure, or other rules that are exempt from the informal rulemaking process. Agencies are not required to accompany such rules with statements of basis and purpose and rarely do so. A court that is called upon to review such a rule through application of the arbitrary and capricious test can remand the rule to the agency with instructions to provide an explanation sufficient to support the rule. In the absence of comments on a proposed rule in which the petitioners criticized the proposed rule, submitted studies that purported to undermine the basis for the rule, and argued in support of alternatives to the proposed rule, however, the petitioners have little chance of success in attempting to persuade a court that the agency's explanation for the rule is so inadequate that the court should characterize it as arbitrary and capricious.

3. *The Record on Review*

As in the case of judicial review of adjudications, courts are not permitted to go beyond the record created by the agency in the process of reviewing an agency rule except in rare circumstances.[63] In the case of a major rulemaking conducted through use of the informal rulemaking process, the record typically is many thousands, or even millions, of pages long. It includes the NOPR, any studies the agency included with the NOPR or incorporated by reference in the NOPR, the comments submitted by the public (often including numerous studies), the final rule, and the statement of basis and purpose. In the case of a rule that is exempt from the informal rulemaking process, the record typically consists of the rule and any statement the agency provided to the court to explain the basis for the rule.

---

61. E.g., Allied–Signal v. NRC, 988 F.2d 146 (D.C. Cir. 1993).

62. E.g., Honeywell International v. EPA, 374 F.3d 1363 (D.C. Cir. 2004) (two judges express the view that the remedy is not lawful or appropriate in any situation.)

63. See § 3E(5).

Chapter Five

STATUTORY CONSTRUCTION IN THE ADMINISTRATIVE STATE

The Supreme Court made a major change in its approach to statutory construction in its landmark 1984 decision in Chevron v. Natural Resources Defense Council.[1] Because of the significance of that decision, this chapter will begin with a description of the pre-*Chevron* legal regime and then describe the post-*Chevron* legal regime.

A. The Pre-*Chevron* Law

Prior to *Chevron*, judicial review of agency constructions of the statutes they implement was characterized by pervasive inconsistency and unpredictability. Two cases decided in 1944 illustrate the problem. In NLRB v. Hearst Publications[2], a five-Justice majority criticized a circuit court for ignoring the NLRB's construction of the term employee, as that term is used in the NLRA and for instead drawing on definitions of the term adopted by courts for use in other contexts like tort law and tax law. The Court upheld the agency's construction of the term and instructed reviewing courts to uphold an agency construction of an agency-administered statute if it has "a reasonable basis in law." The majority explained why such a deferential standard of review was appropriate:

> Everyday experience in the administration of the statute gives [the agency] familiarity with the circumstances and backgrounds of employment relationships in various industries, with the abilities and needs of the workers for self-organization, and with the adaptability of collective bargaining for the peaceful settlement of their disputes with their employers.

During the same Term, however, a six-Justice majority did just what the *Hearst* majority criticized the circuit court for doing—it ignored the agency's construction of a statutory term based on the agency's experience and adopted instead the Court's own interpretation even though the majority admitted that the statute was ambiguous and the agency's construction was entirely plausible.[3]

---

1. 467 U.S. 837 (1984).
2. 322 U.S. 111 (1944).

3. Davies Warehouse Co. v. Bowles, 321 U.S. 144 (1944).

For decades the Court flip-flopped between those diametrically opposed approaches to interpretation of agency-administered statutes, with no explanation of why it used one approach in some cases and the opposite approach in other cases. To confuse the matter still further, the Court announced yet a third standard for reviewing agency interpretations of agency-administered statutes in its 1944 opinion in Skidmore v. Swift & Co.[4]:

> The weight of such a judgment [agency statutory interpretation] in a particular case will depend upon the thoroughness evident in its consideration, the validity of its reasoning, its consistency with earlier and later pronouncements, and all those factors that give it power to persuade, if lacking power to control.

To this day, no one is quite sure what this verbal formulation means. The Court seemed to interpret it as a deferential standard of review in some cases but as a mere description of the Court's openness to potential persuasion in others.

B. The *Chevron* Two–Step

The Court announced a new approach to judicial review of agency statutory constructions in its landmark 1984 opinion in *Chevron*:

> When a court reviews an agency's construction of the statute it administers, it is confronted with two questions. First, always, is the question of whether Congress has directly spoken to the precise question at issue. If the intent of Congress is clear, that is the end of the matter; for the court, as well as the agency, must give effect to the unambiguously expressed intent of Congress. If, however, the court determines Congress has not directly addressed the precise question at issue, the court does not simply impose its own construction on the statute, as would be necessary in the absence of an administrative interpretation. Rather, if the statute is silent or ambiguous with respect to the specific issue, the question for the court is whether the agency's answer is based on a permissible construction of the statute.

This highly deferential test requires a court to uphold any reasonable agency construction of an ambiguous agency-administered statute. In 2007, the Supreme Court held that *Chevron* also applies to agency interpretations of conflicting statutory commands.[5]

---

4. 323 U.S. 134 (1944).

5. National Ass'n of Home Builders v. Defenders of Wildlife, 551 U.S. 644 (2007).

The *Chevron* Court also provided an entirely new justification for its new approach. The Court recognized that giving meaning to an ambiguous term in a statute is a policy decision rather than a legal decision. As such, it should be made by a politically accountable institution and:

> Judges . . . are not part of either political branch of government. In contrast, an agency to which Congress has delegated policymaking responsibility may, within the limits of that delegation, properly rely on the incumbent administration's views of wise policy to inform its judgments. While agencies are not directly accountable to the people, the Chief Executive is, and it is entirely appropriate for this political branch of government to make such policy choices.

In other words, agencies, rather than courts, should interpret ambiguous provisions in agency-administered statutes because that interpretative task actually constitutes policymaking, and policymaking should be undertaken by politically accountable agencies rather than politically unaccountable courts. Under *Chevron,* a court's role is limited to: (1) determining whether the statute is clear or ambiguous with respect to the issue raised, and (2) determining whether the agency policy decision implicit in the construction adopted by the agency is permissible. In other parts of the opinion, the Court equated "permissible" with "reasonable," as opposed to arbitrary and capricious.

While the Court based the *Chevron* test on the need to allocate policymaking to politically-accountable agencies, the test furthers other important goals as well. First, it is entirely consistent with the superior expertise rationale for deferential judicial review the Court recognized in cases like *Hearst.* Second, since there is only one agency and there are thirteen courts of appeal, the deferential *Chevron* test furthers the goals of consistency and coherence by reducing the incidence of circuit splits with respect to the meaning of national statutes.

C. Effects of *Chevron*

The many empirical studies of the effects of *Chevron* find that it has been a qualified success in furthering its goals. Judges still infuse the process of judicial review of agency constructions of agency-administered statutes with their own political and ideological preferences but to a considerably lesser extent than they did in the pre-*Chevron* world.[6] Judges retain some discretion to engage in

---

6. Thomas Miles & Cass Sunstein, Do Judges Make Regulatory Policy? An   Empirical Investigation of *Chevron*, 73 U.Chi. L. Rev. 823 (2006); Richard Re-

policy-making disguised as judicial review of agency constructions of statutes because of the inherent tension between the text of the *Chevron* opinion and footnote nine in which the Court said:

> The judiciary is the final authority on issues of statutory construction and must reject administrative constructions which are contrary to clear congressional intent.... If a court, employing traditional tools of statutory construction, ascertains that Congress had an intention on the precise question at issue, that intention is the law and must be given effect.

Of course, carried to its logical extreme, that statement would leave no room for *Chevron* to play any role, since a court can always use some combination of "traditional tools of statutory construction" to make its own determination of legislative intent. There is general agreement that courts should not use all of the tools of statutory construction to divine the meaning of a statute that is subject to *Chevron* deference, but there is considerable difference of opinion among judges and Justices about which tools are legitimate for this purpose. There is broad agreement that the plain meaning of the language of a statute can trump *Chevron* deference, but judges and Justices sometimes use more debatable and malleable "tools" like canons of construction, legislative purpose, and legislative history as the basis for a judicial construction of a statute that contradicts an agency construction.

D.　Scope of *Chevron*

Chevron deference does not apply to all agency interpretations of agency-administered statutes. It clearly applies to interpretations adopted in notice and comment rulemakings and formal adjudications. Beyond that, it is difficult to generalize. In U.S. v. Mead Corp.,[7] the Court acknowledged that "we have sometimes found reasons for *Chevron* deference even when no such formality was required and none was afforded," but it has not described the less formal circumstances in which *Chevron* deference is appropriate except by reference to one situation in which it concluded that *Chevron* deference was not appropriate. The Court held that *Chevron* deference did not apply to statutory interpretations adopted in tariff classification ruling letters issued by the Customs Service where (1) there was no evidence that Congress intended to give the Service the power to issue classification rulings with the force of

vesz, Environmental Regulation, Ideology and the D.C. Circuit, 83 Va. L. Rev. 1717 (1997); Peter Schuck & Donald Elliott, To the *Chevron* Station: An Empirical Study of Federal Administrative Law, 1990 Duke L.J. 984.

7. 533 U.S. 218 (2001).

law; (2) the rulings rarely give reasons, have no effects on third parties, and have no precedential effect, and (3) 46 offices around the country issue 10,000 to 15,000 such letters each year. If *Chevron* deference does not apply to an agency interpretation, the much weaker form of deference described in *Skidmore* does. (See section A for a discussion of *Skidmore*).

Given the lack of clear guidance from the Supreme Court with respect to the scope of *Chevron*, it should come as no surprise that circuit courts are struggling in their attempts to determine whether *Chevron* applies to an agency interpretation announced in a less formal instrument than a legislative rule or an agency order issued in a formal adjudication.[8] Many circuit courts are performing as well as might be expected in the circumstances, however, by focusing on the pragmatic effects of decisions to apply or not to apply *Chevron* deference. Thus, for instance, the Ninth Circuit provided a good explanation for its decision to accord *Chevron* deference to statutory interpretations adopted in decisions issued by the Board of Immigration Appeals (BIA) but not to statutory interpretations adopted in decisions of individual Immigration Judges (IJ) where the IJ's decision was upheld by BIA in result only with no indication of whether BIA agreed with the reasoning in the IJ decision:

> Where the BIA simply affirms the *results* of an IJ's decision without issuing its own statutory analysis or indicating any intent to create precedent that will bind other IJs or itself, the *Mead* test is not met. After such an affirmance, another IJ could reach the opposite conclusion without violating any established agency position.... The sheer number of IJ decisions underscores our conclusion that they do not carry the force of law and are thus not entitled to *Chevron* deference.... IJs working out of 53 immigration courts located throughout the United States issue hundreds of thousands of decisions annually....[9]

---

8. See Lisa Bressman, How *Mead* Has Muddled Judicial Review of Agency Action, 58 Vand. L. Rev. 1443 (2005).

9. Miranda Alvarado v. Gonzales, 449 F.3d 915 (9th Cir. 2006).

Chapter Six

AGENCY DELAY

A. The Problem

Agency delay is ubiquitous and frustrating to all participants in the administrative process. Agencies routinely take one to two years to act on applications for much needed benefits, such as Social Security disability benefits and Veteran's benefits, and a decade or more to issue a rule that addresses a serious health or safety issue. It is easy to identify the sources of the problem. Congress demands that agencies perform more and more difficult tasks using increasingly burdensome and time-consuming procedures with constantly diminishing resources.[1] The only promising solutions to the problem are equally easy to identify. Ubiquitous delay in agency decisionmaking will continue unless and until Congress reduces the number of tasks it assigns agencies, reduces the scope of the decisionmaking procedures it mandates in statutes, and increases the funds available to agencies. Of course, none of those actions is available to an agency or court, so both institutions simply continue to muddle through with access to legal remedies that are inadequate to the task.

B. Legal Remedies for Delay

1. The APA Remedy

APA § 706(1) instructs a court to compel agency action that is "unreasonably delayed." Of course, the limit on the efficacy of this remedy is apparent upon considering the difficulty of the judicial task of determining that delay is "unreasonable." Even decades of delay in taking a particular action is not unreasonable if the agency simply lacks the resources needed to take all of the actions Congress has instructed it to take. In that universal situation, a court can order an agency to expedite its action in one case only by diverting scarce resources from other cases that may be equally or more urgent in nature than the case that is the subject of the delay petition. That would require a court to reorder an agency's allocation of its scarce resources among competing statutory assign-

---

1. See Richard Pierce, Judicial Review of Agency Actions in a Period of Diminishing Agency Resources, 49 Admin. L. Rev. 61 (1997).

ments—a task that the Supreme Court has cautioned courts not to undertake because they are ill-suited to it.[2] The D.C. Circuit has announced a six-part balancing test that it applies to petitions to compel agency action that is unreasonably delayed.[3] It is difficult for a petitioner to prevail through application of that test, particularly since the Supreme Court admonished circuit courts not to second-guess agency resource allocation decisions. The most a petitioner can expect in most cases is a response from the agency in which it proposes a timetable for action in the case. The court that entertains the petition may then place its imprimatur on the agency timetable, thereby putting pressure on the agency to expedite the matter. In any event, the 706(1) remedy is potentially available only to require an agency to expedite its action in a particular discrete matter where the agency is statutorily required to take the action at issue. The Supreme Court has held that it is not even potentially available as a means of forcing an agency to expedite its implementation of a regulatory program.[4]

2. *Statutory Deadlines*

Another potential remedy for agency delay is a statutory deadline. That remedy avoids the institutional limitations that render the APA remedy largely ineffective. Unlike a politically unaccountable court, Congress has the institutional competence to give an agency legally-binding and judicially-enforceable instructions with respect to its allocation of its scarce resources among its assigned duties. If Congress exercised that power in a thoughtful and responsible manner, statutory deadlines could be a useful means of managing agency delay. Unfortunately, Congress does not set deadlines in that manner. It sets unrealistically short deadlines applicable to most of the tasks it assigns agencies. Thus, for instance, one study found that EPA was then subject to 328 statutory deadlines and that it had been able to comply with only 17% of the deadlines Congress had imposed on it.[5] Every study of statutory deadlines has concluded that they are ineffective and counterproductive.[6]

---

2. See Heckler v. Chaney, 470 U.S. 821 (1985).

3. Telecommunications Research and Action Center v. FCC, 750 F.2d 70 (D.C. Cir. 1984).

4. Norton v. Southern Utah Wilderness Alliance, 542 U.S. 55 (2004).

5. Environmental and Energy Study Institute and Environmental Law Institute, Statutory Deadlines in Environmental Legislation (1985).

6. E.g., Carnegie Commission on Science, Technology, and Government, Risk and the Environment: Improving Regulatory Decisionmaking 58–59 (1993); Shep Melnick, Administrative Law and Bureaucratic Reality, 44 Admin. L. Rev. 245 (1992); Alden Abbott, Case Studies on the Costs and Benefits of Federal Statutory Deadlines, 39 Admin. L. Rev. 467 (1987).

Two circuit court decisions involving the Freedom of Information Act (FOIA) illustrate the frustrations courts experience in grappling with unrealistic statutory deadlines. FOIA requires an agency to respond to an FOIA request within 20 days. Agencies rarely comply with that deadline. Congress originally estimated that compliance with FOIA would cost all agencies a total of $100,000 per year—a tiny fraction of the cost of compliance at any agency—and Congress consistently refuses to appropriate funds sufficient to permit most agencies to comply with the FOIA deadline. In the first case to consider a petition to enforce the FOIA deadline against an agency, the D.C. Circuit refused to do so.[7] It concluded that it was impossible for an agency to comply with the deadline and that entertaining suits to enforce the deadline would have the ineffective and counterproductive effect of forcing everyone who requests information to sue, thereby requiring the agency to engage in a never-ending cycle of reallocation of scarce resources in an unsuccessful attempt to comply with each court order. More recently, the Ninth Circuit expressed frustration with the Department of Justice for its twenty-year delay in responding to an FOIA request, but the court concluded that the source of the problem was the unwillingness of Congress to appropriate adequate funds for this purpose, and the only remedy it could identify was a request that the Department bring the problem to the attention of Congress.[8]

3. Forbidden Remedies

The Supreme Court has rejected two potential remedies for delay. In Heckler v. Day, 467 U.S. 104 (1984), the Court held that a court could not impose a state-wide (or presumably a circuit-wide) deadline on agency decisionmaking in a class of cases. Empirical studies of deadlines of the type the Court rejected found that the deadlines had two effects. First, they forced the agency to reallocate its resources geographically, thereby increasing delay in other locations, and second, they forced the agency to truncate the decisionmaking process to such an extent that the quality of its decisions declined significantly.[9] The Court has also held that a court cannot preclude an agency from taking an action if it has not acted by a

7. Open America v. Watergate Special Prosecution Force, 547 F.2d 605 (D.C. Cir. 1976).

8. Fiduccia v. Department of Justice, 185 F.3d 1035 (9th Cir. 1999).

9. Jerry Mashaw, Bureaucratic Justice 188 (1983).

statutory deadline because Congress did not specify such a draconian consequence for failure to comply with the deadline.[10]

10. Barnhart v. Peabody Coal, 537 U.S. 149 (2003).

Chapter Seven

REVIEWABILITY

A. Presumption of Reviewability

Most statutes that authorize an agency to act also provide explicitly that final actions taken by the agency are (or are not) subject to judicial review, but sometimes Congress is silent or ambiguous with respect to the availability of judicial review of a class of agency actions. In its landmark 1967 opinion in Abbott Laboratories v. Gardner,[1] the Supreme Court announced that a presumption of reviewability applies to all agency actions. The Court attributed the presumption to the Administrative Procedure Act (APA).

> The Administrative Procedure Act ... embodies the basic presumption of judicial review.... So long as no statute precludes such relief or the action is not one committed to agency discretion.... The Administrative Procedure Act provides specifically not only for review of "agency action made reviewable by statute" but also for review of "final agency action for which there is no other adequate remedy in a court," ... [O]nly upon a showing of "clear and convincing evidence" of a contrary legislative intent should courts restrict access to judicial review.

Abbott did not actually involve a reviewability issue. The applicable statute, the Food, Drug & Cosmetics Act, explicitly provided for review of the legislative rule that Abbott sought to challenge. Until the Court decided *Abbott*, however, agency rules were not generally considered ripe for judicial review unless and until the rule was applied. In *Abbott*, the Court changed the ripeness doctrine in significant ways that had the effect of rendering a high proportion of agency rules ripe for review in an abstract, pre-enforcement context. *Abbott*'s important role with respect to the law of ripeness is discussed in § 8C.

The Court applied its newly-announced presumption of reviewability for the first time in the context of an actual reviewability dispute in its 1971 opinion in Citizens to Preserve Overton Park v. Volpe.[2] In *Overton Park*, the Court held reviewable a decision of the

---

1. 387 U.S. 136 (1967).   **2.** 401 U.S. 402 (1971).

Department of Transportation to provide federal funding for a section of an interstate highway that the petitioner alleged to have been routed through a park in a manner that was inconsistent with the Federal Aid to Highways Act. That statute did not provide for judicial review, but the Court applied the presumption of reviewability to support its holding that the decision was reviewable because there was no "clear and convincing evidence" that Congress intended to preclude review. The Court also held that the decision did not fall within the scope of the explicit APA exemption from review applicable to "agency action . . . committed to agency discretion by law." The Court characterized that exemption as "narrow," "rare," and applicable only when there is "no law to apply." The Court concluded that the statute at issue had a justiciable standard in the form of a prohibition on funding roads that go through parks if a feasible and prudent alternative exists.

The presumption of reviewability was never as strong and broad as the rhetoric in *Abbott* and *Overton Park* suggested. Thus, for instance, around the same time that the Court decided *Overton Park*, the First and Second Circuits held that decisions by the Department of Housing and Urban Development to authorize rent increases at federally-subsidized apartment houses were not subject to review.[3] The courts noted that Congress was silent with respect to judicial review of such decisions and expressed skepticism that courts could engage in constructive review of agency decisions to authorize increases in rents.

The presumption of reviewability continues to play a role in reviewability decisions, but it is both weaker and narrower than it once was. Thus, for instance, in its 1984 decision in Block v. Community Nutrition Board,[4] the Supreme Court held that consumers could not obtain judicial review of a decision of the Milk Marketing Board that had the effect of increasing the price of milk. The Court explained that the clear and convincing standard is "not a rigid evidentiary test but a useful reminder to courts that, where substantial doubt about the congressional intent exists, the general presumption favoring judicial review of administrative action is controlling." The Court went on to identify five ways in which the presumption could be rebutted: (1) specific statutory language, (2) specific legislative history, (3) contemporary judicial construction followed by congressional acquiescence, and, most notably, (4) the collective import of the legislative and judicial history of the statute and (5) inferences of intent drawn from consideration of the statute

---

3. Langevin v. Chenango Court, 447 F.2d 296 (2d Cir. 1971); Hahn v. Gottlieb, 430 F.2d 1243 (1st Cir. 1970).

4. 467 U.S. 340 (1984).

as a whole. The following year, the Court reduced the scope of the presumption significantly by holding that it does not apply to agency decisions not to act. That landmark opinion is discussed in the next section of this chapter. Finally, the Court has held that Presidential decisions are not subject to APA review because the President is not an "agency."[5] A presidential decision is subject to only a narrow type of non-statutory review when the President either violates a clear statutory prohibition or deprives an individual of a right conferred by statute or by the Constitution.[6]

1. Statutory Preclusion of Review

When the Court holds that an agency action is not subject to judicial review, it relies on one of two subsections of APA § 701(a). Subsection (a)(1) exempts from review actions where "statutes preclude review." Once the Court identified the five ways in which the presumption of reviewability could be overcome in its opinion in *Block,* lower courts began to use each of the five as ways of supporting an inference that Congress intended to preclude review of various types of agency actions.

2. Committed to Agency Discretion by Law

Subsection (a)(2) exempts from review "agency action . . . committed to agency discretion by law." The Supreme Court has issued several opinions that provide helpful guidance with respect to the meaning of that subsection. Thus, for instance, in its 1988 opinion in Webster v. Doe, the court held that decisions by the Director of the Central Intelligence Agency (CIA) to terminate employees are not subject to judicial review. The Court relied in part on the context in which the agency decision is made, e.g., Congress may have better reasons for conferring unreviewable personnel decision-making discretion on the CIA Director than on the HUD Secretary. It also relied in part on statutory language. The statute authorizes the Director to terminate an employee "in his discretion . . . whenever he shall deem such termination necessary or advisable in the interests of the United States." The Court said that the language of the statute "fairly exudes deference to the Director." A seven-Justice majority went on, however, to hold that the terminated employee could maintain the action he filed against

---

5. Dalton v. Specter, 511 U.S. 462 (1994).

6. E.g., Leedom v. Kyne, 358 U.S. 184 (1958); American School of Magnet- ic Healing v. McAnnulty, 187 U.S. 94 (1902).

the Director in which he argued that the Director had violated his constitutional rights. That holding is illustrative of the powerful tendency of courts to use the avoidance canon to interpret ambiguous statutes in ways that avoid the need to resolve difficult constitutional questions. In the view of the majority, a statute that commits disputes involving alleged infringement of constitutional rights to the unreviewable discretion of an agency would raise serious constitutional questions.

The Supreme Court issued another opinion in 1996 that is particularly helpful in reconciling APA § 701(a)(2), exempting from review agency actions committed to agency discretion, and APA § 706(2)(A), instructing a court to hold unlawful an agency action that is "arbitrary, capricious, an abuse of discretion...." The key is to recognize that, while almost all agency actions involve exercises of agency discretion, only a few are committed to the unreviewable discretion of an agency. Judicially-enforceable limits on agency discretion can emanate from several sources, including mandatory justiciable standards contained in statutes and mandatory justiciable standards contained in legislative rules. In INS v. Yang,[7] the Court held that, while the statute that authorized the Attorney General to waive a deportation order was worded so broadly that the Attorney General had unreviewable discretion initially with respect to such waiver decisions, he had subsequently limited his discretion by announcing and applying "by rule, or by settled course of adjudication, a general policy by which [his] exercise of discretion will be governed." Once an agency so acts, "an irrational departure from that policy (as opposed to an avowed alteration of it) could constitute action that must be overturned as 'arbitrary, capricious, or abuse of discretion'...." The Court has also made it clear, however, that an agency's announced policies do not limit its discretion when they are not mandatory, are stated in hortatory terms, or do not create a standard that is susceptible to judicial application.[8]

B. Presumption of Unreviewability of Agency Inaction

Until 1985, there was disagreement among lower courts on the question whether the presumption of reviewability applies to agency decisions not to act. In Heckler v. Chaney[9], the Supreme Court resolved that dispute definitively by holding that agency inaction is

---

7. 519 U.S. 26 (1996).

8. Your Home Visiting Nurse Services v. Shalala, 525 U.S. 449 (1999).

9. 470 U.S. 821 (1985).

subject to a presumption of unreviewability. The dispute was initiated by a petition filed by opponents of the death penalty in which they urged FDA to begin an investigation to determine whether prescription drugs used by states for purposes of lethal injections were "safe and effective" for that purpose and, if the answer to that question is yes, to declare that it is illegal for states to use the drugs for that purpose. FDA refused to take those actions, and the opponents of the death penalty appealed to a circuit court. The court applied the presumption of reviewability to the agency's decision not to act and then relied on an FDA policy statement to support the court's claim that FDA was obligated to conduct the investigation and to prohibit the use of the drugs for this purpose. The Supreme Court reversed and held that a presumption of unreviewability applies to agency decisions not to act.

The Court analogized to the ancient common law prohibition on judicial review of exercises of prosecutorial discretion. It also acknowledged the reality that no agency can act with respect to all of the alleged violations of law within its jurisdiction and referred to the complicated combination of factors an agency must consider in deciding how to allocate its scarce investigative and prosecutorial resources among competing cases, including severity of effects of violation, likelihood of success, magnitude of required resources, and relationship with overall enforcement program. The Court said that courts are ill-equipped to review such resource allocation decisions and announced the presumption of unreviewability of agency inaction.

The Court referred to one situation in which the presumption is rebutted—when a statute couples the language of command with a justiciable standard. Since the statute at issue in *Chaney* contained only the permissive "may," rather than the mandatory "shall," the Court reversed the circuit court and held that FDA was not required to conduct the requested investigation or enforcement action.

The Court also referred in footnotes to three other situations in which the presumption might be rebutted. First, the Court suggested that an agency decision not to initiate a rulemaking in response to a petition for rulemaking might be reviewable. The Court subsequently held such a decision not to act reviewable.[10] The Court distinguished decisions not to initiate rulemakings from decisions not to initiate investigations or adjudications on three bases—they are less frequent, in § 553 of the APA Congress required each agency to explain why it is not initiating a rulemak-

---

10. Massachusetts v. EPA, 549 U.S. 497 (2007).

ing in response to a petition to do so, and an agency's reasons for not acting in response to a petition for rulemaking are more frequently rooted in legal reasoning that is potentially susceptible to judicial review.

Second, the Court referred to the possibility that the presumption might be rebutted by an agency rule that coupled the language of command with a justiciable standard. The Court concluded that the agency statement that the circuit court had relied on in *Chaney* to provide legal standards a court could apply to the agency decision not to act in that case did not qualify because it was a policy statement rather than a legally binding rule, it did not use the language of command, and it left the agency with discretion whether to act in the circumstances presented. Since the Court decided *Chaney*, it has strongly suggested that a legislative rule that couples the language of command with a justiciable standard is sufficient to overcome the presumption of unreviewability of agency inaction,[11] and every circuit court that has addressed the issue has so held.[12]

Third, the Court referred to the possibility that a court might be justified in reviewing agency inaction when an agency has "consciously and expressly adopted a policy that is so extreme that it represents an abdication of the agency's statutory responsibilities." Cases of that type are so rare, however, that there is no well-developed law on the subject. In 2004, the Second Circuit reported that it had been unable to locate a single post-*Chaney* case of that type, and it concluded that the case before it did not qualify as so extreme that it justified judicial intervention.[13]

In its 2004 opinion in Norton v. Southern Utah Wilderness Alliance,[14] the Supreme Court broadened the presumption of unreviewability of agency inaction by holding that a court cannot compel an agency to act when a statute imposes only a broad duty on the agency and leaves to the agency's discretion the choice of means of fulfilling that duty.

---

11. See INS v. Yang, 519 U.S. 26 (1996), discussed in § 7A(2).

12. E.g., Greater Los Angeles Council on Deafness v. Baldrige, 827 F.2d 1353 (9th Cir. 1987).

13. Riverkeeper, Inc. v. Collins, 359 F.3d 156 (2d Cir. 2004).

14. 542 U.S. 55 (2004).

Chapter Eight

TIMING OF REVIEW

A. Introductory Overview

An agency action cannot be reviewed by a court until it is final, ripe for review, and the petitioner has exhausted administrative remedies. The three doctrines that together determine whether an agency action that is otherwise reviewable is reviewable at the present time and in its present posture differ in their emphasis and in the decisional factors they incorporate. Each is discussed as a discrete doctrine in sections B, C, and D of this chapter. Functionally, however, the three doctrines overlap—whenever the facts and circumstances suggest that one is available, plausible arguments usually can be made with respect to each of the other two. This poses a challenge to a petitioner, since it can only obtain review if it prevails with reference to each of the three doctrines, while the government can delay review of the action at issue—sometimes for years—by prevailing with respect to only one of the three. The functional overlap among the three timing doctrines is illustrated particularly well by the opinions issued by a panel of the D.C. Circuit in 1987 in Ticor Title Insurance Co. v. FTC.[1] Each of the three judges agreed that the agency action at issue was not yet subject to review, but each relied on a different doctrine—the first judge concluded that the action was final and ripe but that the petitioner had not exhausted administrative remedies, the second judge concluded that the action was ripe and that the petitioner had exhausted administrative remedies but that the action was not yet final, while the third judge concluded that the action was final and that the petitioner had exhausted administrative remedies but that the action was not yet ripe for review.

The doctrine discussed in section E, primary jurisdiction, is in a sense the flip side of the three timing doctrines. It is the basis for judicial decisions to refer questions or entire disputes to agencies for initial resolution when a party has raised an issue in a judicial proceeding. Functionally, however, primary jurisdiction also overlaps with the three timing doctrines. Since it too determines the allocation of initial decision-making responsibility between agencies and courts, it should come as no surprise that courts focus on the same decisional factors in making decisions through application of

---

1. 814 F.2d 731 (D.C. Cir. 1987).

the primary jurisdiction doctrine as in making decisions through application of the three timing doctrines.

B. Final Agency Action

Except in the unusual case in which some other statute makes a non-final agency action reviewable, APA § 704 makes only final agency actions reviewable. The Supreme Court announced a two-part test for determining whether an action is final in its 1997 opinion in Bennett v. Spear.[2] "First, the action must mark the 'consummation' of the agency's decisionmaking process.... [S]econd, the action must be one by which 'rights or obligations have been determined' or from which 'legal consequences will flow.'" In *Bennett*, the Court held that a biological opinion issued by the Fish & Wildlife Service (FWS) under the Endangered Species Act was a final agency action. The first part of the test was easy to apply, as often is the case. The agency had unequivocally concluded that a project under consideration for approval by another government agency (referred to by the Court as the action agency) would, without modification, jeopardize the continued existence of an endangered species. The second part of the test was more difficult to apply. FWS had no direct power to approve or disapprove the project at issue. Yet, the Court held that the FWS biological opinion satisfied the second part of the test because it "alter[ed] the legal regime to which the agency action [approval or disapproval of the proposed project] is subject." The Court noted that "action agencies very rarely engage in conduct that [FWS] has concluded is likely to jeopardize the continued existence of a listed species."

The Supreme Court's opinion in Dalton v. Specter[3] illustrates the potential for an agency action to satisfy the first part of the test but to fail the second part. The government conceded that both the Department of Defense (DOD) and the Base Closing Commission (BCC) had made final decisions pursuant to the Base Closing Act (BCA) to close the Philadelphia Navy Yard. The Court held that neither action satisfied the second part of the test for final agency action, however, because the BCA provides that no action taken by DOD or BCC can actually have the effect of closing a base unless and until the President approves the entire list of bases the BCC has proposed to close. The Court went on to hold that the President's action in approving the closure was not reviewable because the President is not an agency within the meaning of the APA and his action was not subject to non-statutory review because it did

---

2. 520 U.S. 154 (1997).   **3.** 511 U.S. 462 (1994).

not deprive an individual of a constitutional or statutory right and did not violate a clear statutory prohibition.[4]

Many regulatory statutes create two-stage sequential decision-making processes that present difficult characterization problems under the final agency action doctrine. Thus, for instance, the Federal Insecticide, Fungicide & Rodenticide Act (FIFRA) provides two ways in which EPA can remove a registered pesticide from the interstate market. It can cancel the registration permanently, or it can suspend the registration temporarily. A cancellation proceeding typically requires years. A registration can only be cancelled by finding that the pesticide's costs exceed its benefits after use of a series of time-consuming decisionmaking procedures. By contrast, a registration can be suspended by making a finding that the pesticide creates an imminent hazard. A suspension proceeding requires few time-consuming or burdensome procedures, so it can be completed relatively quickly. The recurring question for reviewing courts is whether a decision to suspend or not to suspend a registration is a final action taken in a suspension proceeding or a non-final action taken in an ongoing cancellation proceeding. Good arguments can be made on both sides of that issue. A suspension is temporary but it can last for years given the length of a typical cancellation proceeding. During its effective life, a decision to suspend can have severe adverse effects on the manufacturer and users of the pesticide, while a decision not to suspend can have severe adverse effects on public health. The legal standards and evidentiary bases for the two decisions differ, but they overlap. The Supreme Court has never addressed this issue. It should come as no surprise that circuit courts are divided on the issue.[5]

To be final, an agency action must have some legal effect; powerful practical effects are not enough to satisfy the second part of the finality test. This is well-illustrated by the Fourth Circuit's decision in Flue–Cured Tobacco Cooperative Stabilization Corp. v. EPA.[6] EPA issued a report in which it concluded that exposure to second hand smoke greatly increases the risk of contracting lung cancer. The report had powerful adverse effects on cigarette manufacturers and tobacco growers. Numerous states and localities relied on the report as the basis for enacting state statutes and local ordinances that restrict smoking. The Fourth Circuit held, howev-

---

4. See discussion in § 7A.

5. Compare Love v. Thomas, 858 F.2d 1347 (9th Cir. 1988) (suspension order is immediately reviewable final agency action), with Pax Co. v. United States, 454 F.2d 93 (10th Cir. 1972) (suspension order is non-final interlocu-tory action in an ongoing cancellation proceeding that is only potentially reviewable at conclusion of cancellation proceeding.)

6. 313 F.3d 852 (4th Cir. 2002).

er, that the report was not reviewable. It was not final agency action because it had no *direct legal* effects.

In its 2004 opinion in Norton v. Southern Utah Wilderness Alliance,[7] the Supreme Court focused on the "agency action" part of the APA restriction on judicial review to final agency actions. The Court held that only discrete actions, as opposed to broad programs or courses of action, are reviewable.

C. Ripeness

The Supreme Court has long held that an agency action is not reviewable unless and until it is ripe for review. Until 1967, it was extremely difficult to obtain judicial review of an agency rule before the rule was applied in a particular case because courts concluded that a rule rarely is ripe for review unless and until it is applied in a particular case. That difficult-to-meet ripeness standard had enormous practical effects. Most agency rules were never subjected to judicial review. Regulatees and potential applicants for benefits complied "voluntarily" with most rules even when they believed that the rule was invalid.

The alternative of refusing to comply with a rule and then challenging the validity of the rule in a case in which it was applied was viewed as far too risky in the vast majority of cases, since failure to prevail in the effort to challenge the validity of the rule would subject a prospective applicant for benefits to loss of the benefit and a regulatee to criminal and/or civil penalties and costly adverse publicity. Moreover, on the rare occasions when an applicant for benefits or a regulatee challenged a rule in the context of a particular case in which the agency applied it as the basis for a decision denying a benefit or imposing a penalty, the record on which the review proceeding was conducted was the record of the particular case, rather than the record of the rulemaking in which the agency issued the rule. That record typically favored the agency and rendered it unlikely that the petitioner would succeed in its challenge to the validity of the rule. Thus, the adverse consequences of failure in an attempt to challenge the validity of a rule, combined with the high risk of failure, created a powerful deterrent to attempts to obtain judicial review of rules and created a legal environment in which most rules, including many that were probably unlawful, went unchallenged.

---

7. 542 U.S. 55 (2004). See also Lujan v. National Wildlife Federation, 497 U.S. 871 (1990), discussed in § 8C (agency programs are not ripe for review).

That situation changed dramatically with the Supreme Court's issuance of its landmark opinion in Abbott Laboratories v. Gardner.[8] The Court announced a new three-part test of ripeness. While the new test had its most important effects on judicial review of rules, it applies to all agency actions. *Abbott* involved an attempt to obtain pre-enforcement review of a rule (referred to as the every-time rule) in which FDA had required all manufacturers of prescription drugs to include in the labeling and advertising for any drug the typically long and hard to remember generic name of the drug every time the manufacturer mentioned the drug's typically short and easy to remember trade name. The rule was intended to make it easier for doctors to recognize situations in which they could save their patients money by prescribing the typically much cheaper generic equivalent of a drug whose trade name was well-known. Before the Court changed the ripeness test in *Abbott*, it would have held that the FDA rule was not ripe for review unless and until some manufacturer violated it and then challenged its validity in an enforcement proceeding. That was unlikely to happen because a manufacturer would be unlikely to take the chance of incurring civil and/or criminal penalties and significant damage to its public image by refusing to comply and then challenging the rule in an enforcement proceeding.

The Court held the every-time rule ripe for pre-enforcement review by applying a new three-part test: (1) Is there evidence that Congress intended to preclude pre-enforcement of rules issued to implement the statute at issue? (2) Are the issues raised appropriate for judicial resolution at this time and in the abstract context of pre-enforcement review? (3) Would the petitioner suffer hardship if review were deferred until the agency's application of the rule in a particular case allows the court to obtain a better understanding of the rule and its factual components.

The Court stated the first step in the negative, rather than asking whether there was evidence that Congress intended to authorize pre-enforcement review, because of the Court's simultaneous announcement of the powerful presumption of reviewability discussed in § 7A. For the same reason, the Court refused to rely on the existence of a statutorily authorized alternative to pre-enforcement review—review in an enforcement proceeding—as the basis for an inference that Congress intended to preclude pre-enforcement review. The Court went on to conclude that the issue raised by the petitioner with respect to the validity of the every-time rule was appropriate for judicial resolution in an abstract pre-enforcement review proceeding because it involved only an abstract issue of law—did FDA have the statutory authority to issue the

8. 387 U.S. 136 (1967).

106

every-time rule? The Court then concluded that the petitioner would suffer hardship as a result of deferral of review because it would then have to choose between incurring millions of dollars to comply with a rule it believed to be invalid or violating the rule and thereby risking penalties and significant reputational damage if it lost its argument with respect to the validity of the rule in the enforcement proceeding.

The *Abbott* test had the effect of rendering a high proportion of agency rules ripe for pre-application review, but even that permissive test left some rules unripe for review prior to the rule's application in a particular case. The Court's opinion in the companion case of Toilet Goods Ass'n v. Gardner[9] illustrates the circumstances in which a rule was not ripe for pre-enforcement review after *Abbott*. The FDA rule at issue in *Toilet Goods* asserted a right to "free access" to the facilities in which FDA-regulated products are manufactured and stated that FDA "might" deny certification to any manufacturer who denied FDA personnel such "free access." The Court concluded that the issue raised by the petitioner was not appropriate for resolution in an abstract pre-enforcement proceeding. Even though it could be characterized as an issue of law—can FDA assert a right of free access—it raised a series of legal issues the resolution of which depend on the contextual facts, e.g, the circumstances in which the Fourth Amendment authorizes a search of the facilities of a regulatee.

The *Toilet Goods* Court also concluded that the petitioner would not suffer hardship as a result of deferral of review because the only potential consequence of violation of the rule was loss of certification. That part of the opinion should be ignored as unnecessary and disingenuous dicta. It is hard to overstate the devastating effects that loss of certification has on an FDA regulatee—it cannot make any sales in interstate commerce. The D.C. Circuit applies the *Abbott* test pragmatically without looking at all at the consequences of a decision to defer review.[10] The D.C. Circuit recognizes the reality that there is no reason to defer review when an issue raised in a petition can be resolved in an abstract pre-enforcement context and that a court can not resolve an issue that is not appropriate for abstract resolution in a pre-enforcement review proceeding no matter how much hardship the petitioner will suffer as a result of deferral of review.

The contrast between the results of the application of the ripeness test in *Abbott* and *Toilet Goods* illustrates an important

---

9. 387 U.S. 167 (1967).

10. See, e.g., AT & T Corp. v. FCC, 349 F.3d 692 (D.C. Cir. 2003).

point. Most rulemakings raise more than one potential issue. Some issues may be ripe for pre-enforcement review because a court can address the issue as an abstract issue of law, while other issues may not be ripe for pre-enforcement review because a court can address the issue effectively only after the agency has applied the rule to a particular pattern of facts. Of course, arguments that an agency failed to provide a mandatory procedure, such as an adequate notice of proposed rulemaking, an adequate statement of basis and purpose, or an adequate explanation of the action it took, are always ripe for pre-enforcement review. Those are the issues that are raised most frequently in petitions to review rules.

The permissive *Abbott* test of ripeness has had profound effects on the contours of the administrative state. Before *Abbott*, agencies could issue rules quickly and easily; rules were rarely subjected to review; and, agencies prevailed in the vast majority of proceedings that challenged the validity of rules. After *Abbott*, most major rules were subjected to pre-enforcement review; courts began to demand that agencies support rules with lengthy statements of basis and purpose that respond to critical comments and to alternatives proposed in comments and that agencies issue notices of proposed rulemaking that include studies and other data sources on which the agency might rely and that foreshadow all of the potential variants of the rule the agency might adopt; parties to rulemakings responded by submitting voluminous comments that included studies that questioned the validity of the bases for proposed rules and supported alternative rules; courts began to reject thirty to forty per cent of major rules as arbitrary and capricious or on the basis that the notice of proposed rulemaking was inadequate; and, a typical major rulemaking now requires five to ten years to complete and produces a record of at least hundreds of thousands of pages. The transformative effect of *Abbott* and the resulting legal environment is described in § 4B(2).

The Court has cut back on the *Abbott* test in a series of opinions issued between 1990 and 2003. The Court included potentially important dicta in its 1990 opinion in Lujan v. National Wildlife Federation[11] that it turned into part of the basis for a holding in its 2003 opinion in National Park Hospitality Ass'n v. Department of Interior[12]:

> [A] regulation is not ordinarily considered the type of agency action ripe for review ... until the scope of the controversy has been reduced to manageable proportions, and its factual com-

11. 497 U.S. 871 (1990).   **12.** 538 U.S. 803 (2003).

ponents fleshed out by some concrete action applying the regulation to the claimant's situation in a fashion that harms or threatens to harm him.

That statement suggests a presumption against pre-enforcement review of rules, but the Court qualified it and distinguished *Abbott* in a parenthetical:

> (The major exception, of course, is a substantive rule which as a practical matter requires the plaintiff to adjust his conduct immediately.)

In its 1993 opinion in Reno v. Catholic Social Services,[13] the Court suggested that rules governing eligibility for government benefits rarely, if ever, would qualify for pre-application review because, unlike regulatory rules, benefit eligibility rules do not create hardships by imposing penalties on those who violate them.

In its 1994 opinion in Thunder Basin Coal Co. v. Reich,[14] the Court suggested that it was no longer interpreting the first, or statutory, part of the *Abbott* test as it did at the time it decided *Abbott*. The Court referred to the existence of an explicit statutorily-authorized means of obtaining review of a rule and used its existence as the basis for an inference that Congress intended to preclude pre-enforcement review of rules issue to implement the statute. Of course, if the Court had taken that approach to statutory interpretation in *Abbott*, it would have used the explicit availability of review in an enforcement proceeding as the basis for an inference that Congress intended to preclude pre-enforcement review of rules issued to implement the statute at issue in *Abbott*.

Finally, in the three opinions the Court issued in Shalala v. Illinois Long Term Care in 2000, the Justices engaged in an indeterminate debate about the existence of a presumption of reviewability, the strength of any such presumption, and its applicability, if any, to the context of pre-application review of rules. A five-Justice majority stated that any presumption of availability of pre-enforcement review must be "far weaker than a presumption against all review." A dissenting Justice said "Pre-enforcement review is better described as the background rule, which can be displaced by any reasonable implication from the statute." Three other dissenting Justices referred to "our long-standing presumption in favor of pre-enforcement judicial review" but recognized that "the presumption [of reviewability] may not be quite as strong when the question is now-or-later instead of now-or-never."

---

13.   509 U.S. 43 (1993).   **14.**   510 U.S. 200 (1994).

The *Abbott* test, as qualified by the more recent opinions described above, applies not only to rules but to all other agency actions. It has not had major effects in its other applications, however. In fact, in contexts other than pre-application review of rules, it is hard to identify any purpose that ripeness serves that is not served by the final agency action requirement discussed in § 8B. Thus, for instance, informal agency actions, such as letters to regulatees, are held to be ripe if they represent the final views of an agency official with the authority to make a final decision on the matter and if they create rights or duties[15]—decisional criteria that seem indistinguishable from the two-step test for finality the Supreme Court announced in *Bennett*. Similarly, in its 1990 opinion in Lujan v. National Wildlife Federation[16], the court held that petitions to review programs, as opposed to discrete agency actions, are not ripe for review. That reasoning and holding seems functionally indistinguishable from the 2004 opinion in Norton v. Southern Utah Wilderness Alliance[17] in which the Court held that only discrete agency actions can be final agency actions.

D. Exhaustion of Administrative Remedies

The Supreme Court has long held that a party that is dissatisfied with an agency action cannot obtain judicial review of that action unless and until it has exhausted available administrative remedies. That judge-made exhaustion doctrine is discussed in § D1. More recently, Congress has required a prospective petitioner to exhaust particular administrative remedies as a jurisdictional prerequisite to the availability of judicial review of specified types of agency actions. Statutorily-required exhaustion is discussed in § D2. The APA creates special rules applicable to the duty to exhaust intra-agency appeals. Those special rules are discussed in § D3. Finally, as a corollary to the duty to exhaust administrative remedies, courts have long held that an issue cannot be raised in a judicial review proceeding unless the agency was first given an opportunity to address the issue. The requirement of issue exhaustion is discussed in § D4.

15. Compare New York Stock Exchange v. Bloom, 562 F.2d 736 (D.C Cir. 1977) (letter not ripe because views expressed were tentative), with National Automatic Laundry and Cleaning Council v. Shultz, 443 F.2d 689 (D.C. Cir. 1971) (letter ripe because it was from agency head and informed recipients that he had determined they were subject to regulatory requirements of statute.)

16. 497 U.S. 871 (1990).

17. 542 U.S. 55 (2004).

1.　Common Law Exhaustion

In its 1938 opinion in Myers v. Bethlehem Shipbuilding Corp.[18], the Supreme Court rejected an attempt to obtain an injunction that would prohibit an agency from conducting a hearing with reference to a matter that arguably was beyond the agency's jurisdiction with the sweeping assertion that: "[It is] a long-settled rule of judicial administration that no one is entitled to judicial relief for a supposed or threatened injury until the prescribed administrative remedy has been exhausted." That assertion was less than entirely candid when it was made. Just a few years before it decided *Myers*, the Court had announced and applied the "constitutional fact" and "jurisdictional fact" doctrines. The Court held that agencies lacked competence to make findings with respect to any facts on which the constitutionality of an agency action[19] or the jurisdiction of an agency depended[20] and held that courts were required to engage in de novo review of any such agency findings. In that legal environment, courts understandably felt free to enjoin agency actions that they found to be unconstitutional or beyond an agency's jurisdiction. *Myers* was one of several opinions that illustrated the Court's tacit abandonment of the constitutional fact and jurisdictional fact doctrines.[21] After *Myers*, there remain judge-made exceptions to the common law duty to exhaust, but they are quite narrow.

The Supreme Court has identified a long list of powerful reasons for the exhaustion doctrine: It allows agencies to perform the functions Congress assigned them, including fact-finding, applying expertise, and exercising discretion. It enhances efficiency by limiting the occasions when courts must engage in review and permitting agencies to complete their decision-making process prior to judicial intervention. It respects the autonomy of agencies as parts of a branch of government that is separate from the judiciary. It enhances the ability of courts to engage in meaningful review of agency actions by allowing the agency to complete the process of compiling an evidentiary record and explaining why it acted as it did. It reduces the burden on reviewing courts by allowing an agency to dispose of a case on an alternative basis that eliminates the need for a court to resolve a difficult constitutional issue.

18.　303 U.S. 41 (1938).

19.　Ohio Valley Water Co. v. Ben Avon Borough, 253 U.S. 287 (1920).

20.　Crowell v. Benson, 285 U.S. 22 (1932).

21.　Modern courts engage in deferential review of agency findings of con-stitutional and jurisdictional facts except in the unique context of allegations that an agency action violated the First Amendment. See Henry Monaghan, Constitutional Fact Review, 85 Colum. L. Rev. 229 (1985).

Notwithstanding the good reasons that support the exhaustion requirement, the Supreme Court has always recognized the existence of some narrow exceptions. Thus, for instance, a petitioner can be excused from exhausting an administrative remedy by demonstrating that pursuit of an administrative remedy would be an exercise in futility, but the futility exception requires a petitioner to prove that denial of relief through pursuit of the remedy at issue is a certainty, rather than merely highly likely.[22] Similarly, a petitioner can obtain an injunction against an agency action without first exhausting available remedies on the basis that the agency action is beyond the agency's jurisdiction, but only if the agency is "clearly" acting beyond its delegated power and the petitioner has no means of effectively protecting its rights except through immediate judicial intervention.[23]

The Supreme Court has sometimes held that a petitioner can obtain judicial review of the constitutionality of an agency's decision-making procedure without first exhausting the procedure it is challenging.[24] The Court's opinions on that important question are inconsistent, however.[25] The better-reasoned opinions require exhaustion both because an agency usually has the power to change its procedures to bring them in conformance with the Constitution and may do so in response to an argument that its procedures are unconstitutional[26] and because the agency may resolve the case on an alternative basis that avoids the need for a court to resolve the constitutional question.[27]

Two Supreme Court opinions that resolve superficially similar cases in opposite ways illustrate both the importance the Court attaches to the common law exhaustion requirement and its willingness to excuse a petitioner's failure to exhaust in an extreme case. Both cases arose in the context of the Vietnam War era draft system in which a classification of 1–A was often followed by an induction notice ordering the individual to report for basic training followed by a tour of duty in a dangerous and unpopular war. The draft was administered by the Selective Service Administration. The classification process began when the individual completed a questionnaire and submitted it to his local Selective Service office. If the individual was dissatisfied with the classification decision of

---

22. See, e.g., Marine Mammal Conservancy v. Department of Agriculture, 134 F.3d 409 (D.C. Cir. 1998); Greene v. Meese, 875 F.2d 639 (7th Cir. 1989).

23. Leedom v. Kyne, 358 U.S. 184 (1958).

24. E.g., Mathews v. Eldridge, 424 U.S. 319 (1976).

25. See, e.g., W.E.B. DuBois Clubs v. Clark, 389 U.S. 309 (1967).

26. E.g., Barron v. Ashcroft, 358 F.3d 674 (9th Cir. 2004).

27. E.g., PUC v. United States, 355 U.S. 534 (1958).

the local office, he could take advantage of an elaborate multi-step review process.

Some young men chose to protest the draft, however, by refusing even to complete the questionnaire. In such circumstances, the local board had no choice but to classify them 1–A, a decision that became final when they refused to take advantage of the opportunity to appeal the classification decision of the local board. In many such cases, the individual then received an induction notice, refused to comply, and was indicted for the felony of refusing to report for basic training. Two young men—McKart and McGee—found themselves in this situation and decided belatedly to contest their 1–A classifications in the criminal proceeding in which they were charged with refusal to comply with an induction notice. In each case, the government argued that the individual could not raise the misclassification argument because he had not exhausted administrative remedies by contesting his classification in the original classification proceeding or in an intra-agency appeal of the original classification decision.

The Court excused McKart's failure to exhaust.[28] He submitted evidence that he was exempt from the draft as a sole surviving son—his brothers had been killed in the service of their country. The Court reasoned that McKart's failure to exhaust should be excused because incarceration is a high penalty to pay for a failure to exhaust administrative remedies; he clearly was exempt; and, no purpose would have been served by agency consideration of his claim because there was no fact-finding, application of expertise, or exercise of discretion involved in applying the sole surviving son exception. The Court refused to excuse McGee's failure to exhaust, however, even though the consequence of his failure to exhaust was also incarceration for commission of a felony. McGee claimed to be exempt as a conscientious objector.[29] The Court reasoned that his failure to exhaust should not be excused because the agency should have been given an opportunity to engage in the fact-finding, application of expertise, and exercise of discretion inherent in applying the conscientious objector exemption to any individual.

2.   *Statutory Exhaustion*

Sometimes Congress explicitly requires exhaustion as a prerequisite to the availability of judicial review. Thus, for instance, both complaints of violations of civil rights made by prison inmates and

28. McKart v. United States, 395 U.S. 185 (1969).

29. McGee v. United States, 402 U.S. 479 (1971).

claims for reimbursement made by Medicare or Medicaid beneficiaries are subject to detailed and explicit exhaustion requirements. In such cases, no court can excuse a failure to exhaust on any basis.[30]

3. Intra–Agency Appeals

Most agencies provide opportunities for intra-agency appeals of initial agency decisions to higher authorities within the agency. APA § 704 explicitly provides for this common situation:

> Except as otherwise expressly required by statute, agency action otherwise final is final [and hence immediately reviewable] ... whether or not there has been presented or determined an application for a declaratory order, for any form of reconsideration, or, unless the agency otherwise requires by rule and provides that the action meanwhile is inoperative, for an appeal to superior agency authority.

In its 1993 opinion in Darby v. Cisneros,[31] the Court applied that provision as the basis for its holding that an agency could not define a decision as final agency action, allow the action to have an immediate effect, provide an opportunity for an intra-agency appeal of the action, and then succeed in arguing that a party who is adversely affected by such a decision can not obtain review of the decision until it has made use of the intra-agency appeal process the agency made available. In order to make an intra-agency appeal process a mandatory prerequisite to judicial review of an otherwise final action the agency must issue a rule in which it makes the intra-agency appeal process a mandatory prerequisite to the availability of review and in which it provides that the action cannot become effective during the pendency of the intra-agency appeals process. *Darby* and the quoted language from APA § 704 have limited effect, however, because they apply only to actions that are otherwise final (see § 8B), and an agency can make an intra-agency appeal process mandatory simply by issuing a rule that complies with § 704.

4. Issue Exhaustion

In its unanimous 2004 opinion in Department of Transportation v. Public Citizen[32], the Supreme Court reaffirmed and applied a long-standing corollary to the exhaustion requirement—a reviewing court can not consider an issue that the agency was not provided an

---

30. Woodford v. Ngo, 548 U.S. 81 (2006).

31. 509 U.S. 137 (1993).

32. 541 U.S. 752 (2004).

opportunity to consider. In its 2000 opinion in Sims v. Apfel[33], the Court recognized an exception to the requirement that a petitioner first provide the agency an opportunity to consider an argument. The court held that the issue exhaustion rule does not apply to proceedings to determine whether an applicant is eligible to receive Social Security disability benefits because those proceedings are inquisitorial rather than adversarial and the agency has an affirmative statutory duty to develop the facts in each case.

E.   Primary Jurisdiction

The primary jurisdiction doctrine does not arise in proceedings before agencies. Instead, it is invoked by a court at the behest of a party that convinces the court that it should refer an entire case or an issue that has arisen in a case before the court to an agency to allow the agency to decide the case or to resolve the issue initially, subject to potential judicial review. The doctrine can refer to either of two situations. In the first situation, the argument is that the court should dismiss the case before it because only an agency has jurisdiction to resolve the dispute. In that situation, the court's task is simply to interpret the relevant statute to determine whether Congress conferred on an agency exclusive jurisdiction to resolve a dispute of the type that is before the court. If the court decides that Congress made that decision, it must dismiss the case. Thus, for instance, the Supreme Court held in 1907 that a court must dismiss a complaint in which a shipper alleged that a rail rate was unjust and unreasonable because Congress had recently enacted a statute in which it gave the Interstate Commerce Commission exclusive jurisdiction to adjudicate all such disputes.[34]

In the second situation, the primary jurisdiction doctrine arises in a case that is properly before a court but in which a party persuades the court that it can not decide the case without resolving an issue that is more appropriately resolved initially by an agency. In that more common situation, the doctrine has nothing to do with jurisdiction in any technical sense. It provides a pragmatic means of allocating initial decision-making responsibility among institutions in a manner that is likely to produce a higher quality pattern of decisions. If the court invokes primary jurisdiction in that type of case, it refers the issue to the agency and stays its proceedings until the agency has addressed the issue. Thus, for instance, in a 1956 opinion, the Supreme Court held that a court should hold in abeyance a proceeding in which a shipper sued a

33.   530 U.S. 103 (2000).

34.   Texas & Pac. Ry. v. Abilene Cotton Oil Co., 204 U.S. 426 (1907).

railroad for damages for breach of contract where the amount of the damages depended on which of two conflicting tariff provisions applied to the cargo and where the Court concluded that the ICC should make the initial determination of which tariff provision applied to the cargo.[35] In that opinion, the Court described the doctrine:

> No fixed formula exists for applying the doctrine of primary jurisdiction. In every case the question is whether the reasons for existence of the doctrine are present and whether the purposes it serves will be furthered by its application in the particular litigation.

Courts invoke the doctrine when the question to be resolved is complicated and requires the application of expertise of the type possessed by the agency, and where it is particularly important to obtain national uniformity in resolving the question. In contrast, courts tend not to invoke the doctrine where it is relatively easy for a lay court to resolve it, or where the agency has already addressed the issue in ways that a court can ascertain and apply.

Courts have shown an increased tendency to recognize potential delay in the agency decision-making process as a factor mitigating against invocation of the primary jurisdiction doctrine. That potential sometimes induces a court to use an alternative means of attempting to obtain an agency's views on an issue, such as a request for an amicus brief from the agency,[36] or to attach a time limit on the amount of time the court is willing to hold the proceedings in abeyance while it awaits an agency resolution of the referred issue.[37] In 2011, the Supreme Court explicitly approved of the judicial practice of deferring to agency interpretations of agency rules announced in amicus briefs.[38] That increasingly common practice has largely replaced the invocation of the primary jurisdiction doctrine.

---

35. United States v. Western Pacific R.R. Co., 352 U.S. 59 (1956).

36. E.g., Belknap, Inc. v. Hale, 463 U.S. 491 (1983).

37. E.g., Wagner & Brown v. ANR Pipeline Co., 837 F.2d 199 (5th Cir. 1988).

38. Chase Bank v. McCoy, ___ U.S. ___, 131 S.Ct. 871 (2011).

Chapter Nine

STANDING

A. Introductory Overview

The law governing standing to obtain judicial review of agency actions answers only one question—who can obtain review of an otherwise reviewable agency action. It should be a relatively simple, readily accessible area of law. It is the opposite. The Supreme Court has issued over 650 opinions in which it has resolved over 300 standing disputes. The opinions are characterized by complexity and inconsistency. Standing law has become so politicized that it is easier for a political scientist than a lawyer to predict the outcome of a standing dispute. A political scientist can refer to just a few simple and reliable predictors of the outcome of a standing dispute, e.g., conservative Justices always vote to confer standing on business associations and not on individuals who rely on environmental injuries. By contrast, lawyers can refer only to highly malleable doctrines that can be, and have been, interpreted to have a wide variety of meanings in different contexts.[1] Since this book is written for lawyers and law students, however, it will focus on the legal doctrines that comprise the law of standing.

The modern law of standing began with the Supreme Court's landmark 1970 opinion in Association of Data Processing v. Camp (ADP).[2] The Court announced a two-part test to determine whether a petitioner has standing to obtain review of an agency action. The first step is based on the Court's interpretation of Article III of the Constitution. A petition for review creates a case or controversy within the jurisdiction of a court only if "the plaintiff alleges that the challenged action has caused him injury in fact, economic or otherwise." The second part of the test is based on the Court's interpretation of the APA. After recognizing that Congress can resolve the standing question "one way or another, save as the requirements of Article III dictate otherwise," the Court interpreted the APA to confer standing on any petitioner who seeks to protect an interest that is "arguably within the zone of interests to be protected or regulated by the statute or constitutional guarantee in question." The constitutional part of the *ADP* test is discussed in section B. Section B4 discusses an important element of the law of

1. Richard Pierce, Is Standing Law or Politics? 77 N.C.L. Rev. 1714 (1999).

2. 397 U.S. 150 (1970).

standing that was implicit in *ADP* and that arises in a high proportion of standing disputes—standing of associations to represent the interests of their members. The statutory part of the test is discussed in section C.

B. Constitutional Limits on Standing

In order to satisfy the case or controversy restriction on the jurisdiction of federal courts, the agency action that is the subject of the petition for review must cause injury in fact to the petitioner, and that injury must be redressable by a court. Each of these terms—injury in fact, causation, and redressability—is a term of art that can be, and has been, interpreted in a variety of ways by the Court. In subsections 1, 2, and 3, we will describe the ways in which the Court has interpreted each of the three critical terms. In section 4, we will discuss the closely related doctrine of associational standing. In section 5, we will try to make the meaning of the three terms more accessible by discussing the ways in which the Court has interpreted them in each of four contexts—economic injuries, environmental injuries, informational injuries, and procedural injuries.

1. Injury in Fact

Not all injuries qualify as injuries in fact for standing purposes. "Concrete" and "particularized" injuries count, while "abstract" or "generalized" injuries do not. The Justices agree with respect to some parts of the meanings of these terms. Thus, for instance, all agree that injury in the form of anger at the government for violating the law is too abstract to qualify as an injury for standing purposes. The Justices disagree with respect to other important aspects of the meaning of these terms, however. One of the most important areas of disagreement is with respect to "injuries shared by the many." The Court sometimes says that such injuries qualify for standing purposes and sometimes says that they do not. A 2007 standing dispute discussed in § 5b produced a five-to-four division on that question.[3] The question arises with considerable frequency in the context of environmental injuries and informational injuries, so the disagreements among the Justices will be discussed in detail in §§ 5b and c.

All Justices are reluctant to recognize for standing purposes injuries that stem from arguable violations of provisions of the Constitution that are not specifically designed to protect individual

---

3. Massachusetts v. EPA, 549 U.S. 497 (2007).

rights. Thus, for instance, the Court held that taxpayers and voters lack standing to challenge the constitutionality of the longstanding practice of many members of Congress to retain their reserve commissions in the armed forces even though that practice arguably violates the provision in Article I, Section 6 that provides: "no Person holding any Office under the United States shall be a member of either House during his Continuance in Office."[4] Some, but not all, Justices take a different attitude toward injuries that are arguably "abstract" or that are "shared by the many," depending on whether Congress has enacted a statute that appears to recognize the injury at issue. A pair of cases involving informational injuries illustrate that point of disagreement particularly well,[5] so it will be discussed in § 5c.

2. *Causation*

Not all causal relationships between a challenged agency action and an alleged injury to a petitioner qualify for standing purposes. To qualify, a causal relationship must be "actual or imminent," "real and immediate", or "certainly impending," and not "insubstantial," "tenuous," "remote," or "speculative." The Court has not applied those adjectives in a consistent manner, however. Thus, for instance, in *ADP* and the many other economic injury cases, the Court applied a probabilistic test that is easy to meet. If an agency has taken an action that permits a new class of competitors to enter a market in competition with incumbents, the Court draws the logical inference that each incumbent is likely to suffer injury in the form of likely loss of business to the new competitors or reduced prices due to the new competition. Yet, when the Court does not want to resolve a dispute on the merits or to authorize judicial intervention in a class of disputes, the Court applies a highly particularized version of the causation test that is impossible to meet.

Thus, for instance, in the 1984 case of Allen v. Wright,[6] when parents of african-american children sought review of IRS's method of enforcing the statutory and constitutional prohibition on providing tax benefits to schools that discriminate based on race, a majority of Justices held that the parents lacked standing because they had not established that "any particular school" would cease engaging in racial discrimination or increase its tuition if it lost its

---

4. Schlesinger v. Reservists Committee to Stop the War, 418 U.S. 208 (1974).

5. Compare FEC v. Akins, 524 U.S. 11 (1998), with United States v. Richardson, 418 U.S. 166 (1974).

6. 468 U.S. 737 (1984).

favorable tax status, that "any particular parent" of a white child enrolled in such a racially discriminatory school would remove the child from the school in response to an increase in tuition caused by loss of the school's favorable tax status, or that "any particular community" in which one of the petitioners lived would experience enough resulting transfers from racially discriminatory schools to enhance any of the petitioner's children's opportunity to obtain a public education in a racially desegregated school. Of course, as the dissenting opinion pointed out, it is impossible for anyone to prove the existence of a causal relationship between an agency action and an injury through application of the version of the causation test the majority applied. Moreover, if the majority had applied the logical probabilistic version of the standing test it routinely applies in economic injury cases, it would have concluded easily that there was a sufficient causal relationship between the challenged agency action and the alleged injury. That would require only that the Court apply a behavioral postulate that everyone understands and accepts—the behavior of individuals and institutions is affected by the tax consequences of that behavior.

The real reason the *Allen* majority did not want to intervene in the case is easy to infer from the nature of the challenged action— the petitioner sought judicial review of the adequacy of the particular methods the agency had chosen in its efforts to enforce a statutory prohibition that Congress had assigned the agency to enforce. The majority did not want to authorize courts to become involved in agency decisions about the best ways of enforcing laws entrusted to the agencies because courts lack the competence to make such judgments. The Court turned that important principle into a holding a year later in its landmark opinion in Heckler v. Chaney,[7] discussed in § 7B, but apparently there were not five Justices willing to announce that principle a year earlier in the context of the *Allen* case.

The Justices often differ with respect to their assessments of the adequacy of a causal relationship between a challenged action and an alleged injury. Those differences arise with considerable frequency in the context of the environmental injury cases discussed in § 5b. In a 2007 decision that is discussed in § 5b, the Justices divided five-to-four on the question of whether there is sufficient evidence of a causal relationship between emissions of carbon dioxide by automobiles in the U.S. and global warming.[8]

7. 470 U.S. 821 (1985).

8. Massachusetts v. EPA, 549 U.S. 497 (2007).

3. *Redressability*

An injury to a petitioner cannot be the basis for standing unless it can be redressed by a court. In most cases, causation and redressability overlap completely, i.e., if the injury was caused by the challenged agency action, a court order rejecting the action will redress the injury. In some cases, however, some Justices conclude that a court cannot redress a petitioner's injury even if the injury was caused by the challenged action. The Justices divided with respect to such redressability disputes in four environmental injury cases that are discussed in § 5b.[9]

4. *Standing of Associations*

A high proportion of all petitions to review agency actions are filed by member organizations—trade associations, unions, or public interest organizations. An association can have standing as a result of an injury it suffers as an association. Thus, for instance, if an agency authorized a utility to increase the price of electricity an association must pay, the association would suffer an injury caused by the agency action and redressable by a court decision reversing the agency action. Most of the time, however, an association claims standing derivative of the standing of one of its members. The Supreme Court announced a three-part test for determining whether an association has standing to assert the interests of its members in Hunt v. Washington State Apple Advertising Com'n:[10]

> [A]n association has standing to bring suit on behalf of its members when: (1) its members would otherwise have standing to sue in their own right; (2) the interests it seeks to protect are germane to the organization's purpose; and (3) neither the claim asserted nor the relief requested requires the participation of individual members in the lawsuit.

As a practical matter, the second and third parts of the test rarely present problems in the context of petitions to review agency actions, so any controversy about an association's standing usually focuses exclusively on the question whether a member has standing. That question typically is resolved through judicial consideration of affidavits submitted by one or more members.

9. Massachusetts v. EPA, 549 U.S. 497 (2007); Friends of the Earth v. Laidlaw Environmental Services, 528 U.S. 167 (2000); Steel Co. v. Citizens for a Better Environment, 523 U.S. 83 (1998); Lujan v. Defenders of Wildlife, 504 U.S. 555 (1992).

10. 432 U.S. 333 (1977).

During the Reagan Administration, the government argued that associations should not have standing to assert the interests of their members because only injured individuals have sufficient interest in the outcome of a dispute to create a case or controversy. The Supreme Court rejected that argument in 1986.[11] Many people believe that the associational standing doctrine is particularly important because it provides one of the few potential correctives for the well-documented and common collective action problem that confers major advantages on a small group of people, each of whom has a large amount at stake, when they confront a much larger number of people, each of whom has a small amount at stake.[12]

5. *Injury, Causation, and Redressability in Context*
a. Economic Injuries

The Supreme Court has decided many cases with facts nearly identical to the facts of *ADP*, always with the same result—the Court applied easy to meet tests of injury, causation, and redressability, and held that the petitioner has standing. In *ADP*, an agency had taken an action that had the effect of allowing a new class of competitors, banks, to enter a market, provision of data processing services, in competition with incumbents, many of whom were members of the trade association that sought review of the agency action. The Court concluded that the incumbent members of petitioner were likely to suffer economic injury in the form of either loss of customers to the new participants in the market or reduced prices attributable to the need to match the prices of the new participants, and that a court order rejecting the agency action would redress that injury.

b. Environmental Injuries

The Supreme Court's treatment of environmental injuries has been much more variable and has produced much more disagreement among the Justices. In dicta in *ADP*, the Court referred to the injuries that could support standing as "economic or otherwise" and added that the injury could reflect "aesthetic, conservational, or recreational as well as economic values." Two years later, in Sierra Club v. Morton,[13] the Court refused to confer standing on an

---

11. International Union, UAW v. Brock, 477 U.S. 274 (1986).

12. That problem is described well in Mancur Olsen, The Logic of Collective Action: Public Goods and the Theory of Groups (1965).

13. 405 U.S. 727 (1972).

organization simply because it claimed to have an interest in protecting the environment. The Court included in its opinion dicta that indicated the Court's receptivity to petitions for review filed by individuals, or by organizations that include individuals among their members, if the individual, or any member of the organization, alleges that it has suffered an injury to an environmental interest:

> Aesthetic and environmental well-being, like economic well-being, are important ingredients of the quality of life in our society, and the fact that particular environmental interests are shared by the many rather than by the few does not make them less deserving of legal protection through the judicial process.

Between 1972 and 1990, the Court issued several opinions in which it converted its dicta in *ADP* and *Sierra Club* into holdings. It held that a petitioner who alleged an environmental injury caused by an agency action had standing to obtain review of that action. The Court applied versions of the injury in fact, causation, and redressability tests that were extremely easy to meet.[14]

In 1990, the Court issued the first in a series of opinions in which it cut back on the availability of standing based on environmental injuries. Justice Scalia, who joined the Court in 1986, played a prominent role in that effort. Before he joined the Court, he expressed his then-idiosyncratic but strongly held views on this subject in a 1983 law review article.[15] He argued that it was unconstitutional for a court to allow any individual petitioner to assert an interest in environmental protection or to grant standing to an individual to enforce an environmental statute because environmental laws protect public rights that the Take Care Clause in Article II allows only the President to enforce. Justice Scalia has

---

14. E.g., Japan Whaling Ass'n v. American Cetacean Society, 478 U.S. 221 (1986) (whale watchers had standing to obtain review of agency decision that had the potential to reduce the number of whales available to be watched); Duke Power Co. v. Carolina Environmental Study Group, 438 U.S. 59 (1978) (potential thermal degradation of two lakes near homes of petitioners as a result of potential construction of a nuclear powerplant was sufficient to confer standing on petitioners to challenge validity of statute that conferred partial tort immunity on owners of nuclear powerplants where powerplant al-

legedly would not be built without partial tort immunity); United States v. Students Challenging Regulatory Agency Procedures, 412 U.S. 669 (1973) (law students had standing to obtain review of decision to increase rail rates applicable to scrap metal on theory that students would suffer from the effects of increased air pollution caused by substitution of primary metal for recycled metal in some applications).

15. Antonin Scalia, Standing as an Essential Element of Separation of Powers, 17 Suffolk L. Rev. 881 (1983).

put a lot of energy into his attempt to make his views the law, with uneven and uncertain effects.

The Court's first opinion that cut back on environmental standing had an important but modest effect. In its 1990 opinion in Lujan v. National Wildlife Federation (NWF), the Court held that a petitioner who owned land "in the vicinity" of a large tract of public land that might be opened for development as a result of an agency action lacked standing to obtain review of the action. *NWF* established a requirement that a petitioner must have geographic proximity to an environmental injury to be able to use it as the basis to challenge an action that causes the injury.

The Court's second opinion that cut back on the availability of environmental standing was far more drastic in its potential effects. In a plurality opinion issued in 1992 in Lujan v. Defenders of Wildlife (Defenders),[16] the Court concluded that an organization lacked standing to obtain review of a decision of the Fish & Wildlife Service (FWS) to refuse to apply the Endangered Species Act (ESA) to decisions by the Agency for International Development (AID) to provide aid to two overseas projects—in Egypt and Sri Lanka, respectively—that allegedly threatened to take the critical habitat of endangered species—the nile crocodile and the asian leopard, respectively. FWS based its decision on a rule issued by the Department of Interior stating that ESA does not apply outside the U.S. Defenders based its claim of standing on the affidavits of two members, each of whom studies one of the endangered species affected by the projects, each of whom had visited the habitat of the species in the past, and each of whom expressed an intent to visit that habitat again in the future.

Justice Scalia's opinion for a plurality of four Justices stated many reasons in support of the holding that Defenders lacked standing. First, it rejected out of hand three theories propounded by Defenders—(1) ecosystem nexus, i.e., anyone has standing to assert an interest in the preservation of any species because extinction of any species has adverse ripple effects throughout the ecosystem; (2) animal nexus, i.e., anyone who has a special interest in observing a species has an interest in preservation of the species so that he can have an opportunity to observe it in the future; and, (3) professional nexus, i.e, anyone who makes a living as a result of a species has an interest in preservation of that species. Second, it concluded that the Take Care Clause of Article II precludes a court from granting standing to an individual who seeks to enforce an environmental law because such a judicial decision would have the

---

16. 504 U.S. 555 (1992).

effect of interfering with the President's exclusive power to enforce public laws. Third, it concluded that any injury suffered by the petitioners was not judicially redressable because any judicial decision would bind only FWS and would leave AID free to provide the funding anyway. Fourth, it concluded that any injury suffered by petitioners was not judicially redressable because the foreign governments might decide to go forward with the projects as planned rather than to accept any mitigating conditions that FWS might recommend and that AID might apply to implement ESA. Fifth, the concurring opinion concluded that the affidavits submitted by the two members were insufficient because they referred only to their plans to visit the affected habitat at some unspecified time in the future.

The meaning of the decision in *Defenders* is unclear because only four Justices joined the plurality opinion. That opinion produced a holding that Defenders lacked standing because of the concurring opinions of two Justices. The two concurring Justices stated that they did not agree with much of the reasoning in the concurring opinion, however, so it is impossible to know which of the many strands of reasoning in the plurality opinion represent the views of a majority. It is safe to assume that the concurring Justices agreed with the plurality's conclusion that the affidavits submitted were inadequate because they did not specify a time in the near future when the two planned to visit the critical habitat. Thus, it is fair to assume that *Defenders* added a temporal proximity requirement to the geographic proximity requirement the Court announced in *NWF*. Beyond that, however, it is simply not possible to know whether any of the other four reasons given in the plurality opinion were embraced by a majority of Justices.

The Supreme Court's 1998 opinion in FCC v. Akins[17] involved an informational injury, rather than an environmental injury, so it is discussed in greater detail in the next section. The opinion is worth noting in the context of environmental standing, however, because the *Akins* majority held that an individual can assert a judicially cognizable injury even though that injury is shared in common with millions of other people—an issue that arises with considerable frequency in environmental standing cases. Three Justices dissented on that issue.

In its 1998 opinion in Steel Co. v. Citizens for a Better Environment,[18] the Supreme Court relied on redressability as the basis for another decision that had the potential to cutback signifi-

17. 524 U.S. 11 (1998).   **18.** 523 U.S. 83 (1998).

cantly on the availability of environmental standing. *Steel Co.* was not an APA case involving review of an agency action. It was one of the many "citizen suit" cases that are filed to enforce environmental laws. Many federal environmental regulation statutes have provisions that authorize any citizen or any person to bring an action for injunctive relief and/or civil penalties against anyone who violates a statutory prohibition or an agency rule. The defendant conceded that it had violated a prohibition in a federal statute and that its violation had caused injury to a member of the complaining association. Yet, the *Steel Co.* majority held that the plaintiff lacked standing because its injury was not redressable by a court. Injunctive relief was not available against the defendant because it had ceased violating the statute by the time the complaint was filed, and the majority concluded that civil penalties would not redress the plaintiff's injury because they are payable to the government rather than to the plaintiff.

The Supreme Court's 2000 opinion in Friends of the Earth v. Laidlaw Environmental Services adopted an extremely narrow interpretation of *Steel Co.* and appeared to reopen the courthouse doors widely to suits based on environmental injuries. *Laidlaw* was another citizen suit case. As in *Steel Co.*, injunctive relief was not available against the defendant, although for a different reason. While the violation was ongoing at the time the complaint was filed, the defendant had ceased violating the statute by the time the judge decided the case. A seven-Justice majority refused to apply the *Steel Co.* holding and reasoning, however. The *Laidlaw* majority distinguished *Steel Co.* as the unusual case in which the violation at issue was wholly past when the complaint was filed. It held that civil penalties can redress a plaintiff's injury in all other cases because they have the potential to deter future violations that have the potential to cause future injury to the plaintiff. More broadly, the majority instructed courts to defer to any congressional decision that a remedy can redress an injury by deterring future violations of the law.

The *Laidlaw* majority also addressed other important issues that arise with great frequency in the context of environmental injuries. The plaintiff organization claimed standing based on affidavits in which members stated that they had ceased boating, swimming, and fishing in the river downstream of the location in which the defendant had emitted mercury in violation of the Clean Water Act because they feared that defendant's emissions had created unhealthy levels of pollution in the areas in which they previously boated, swam, and fished. The district judge conducted a hearing in which he instructed the parties to present evidence to determine whether the defendant's illegal emissions actually had caused the water where the affiants used the river to be unhealthy. The judge found that the illegal emissions had not caused unhealthy conditions in those locations. The defendant argued that the judge's finding should yield a holding that the plaintiff lacked standing because the defendant's conduct did not actually cause harm to the health of any affiant. Before the Court decided *Laidlaw*, defendants regularly demanded hearings of this type and often used the resulting finding to support a holding that the plaintiff lacked standing. It is virtually impossible to prove that particular illegal emissions caused particular adverse health effects downstream (or downwind) of the location of the illegal emissions. *Laidlaw* put an end to that standard practice.

The *Laidlaw* majority held that an environmental plaintiff need establish only that it (or one of its members) changed its behavior as a result of "reasonable concerns" that the defendant's violations created unhealthy conditions. The two dissenting Justices complained that the opinion of the *Laidlaw* majority "makes the injury-in-fact requirement a sham. If there are ... violations, and a member ... lives near the offending plant. It would be difficult not to satisfy today's lenient standard." *Laidlaw* appeared to reflect a situation in which a clear majority of the Justices once again welcomed suits based on environmental injuries. As so often is the case in standing law, however, the legal environment changed again just a few years later.

In 2007, the Supreme Court addressed an extremely high stakes and high visibility environmental standing dispute in Massachusetts v. EPA.[19] Many environmental organizations, states, and localities sought review of an EPA decision rejecting a petition for rulemaking and refusing to begin a rulemaking to regulate emissions of global warming gases (basically carbon dioxide) by automobiles sold in the U.S. After holding that the action was reviewable (see discussion in § 7B), a five-Justice majority held that Massachusetts had standing to obtain review of the action. There were many petitioners that alleged injuries of various types, but the Justices discussed only land loss by Massachusetts.

The Justices disagreed with respect to virtually every element of the law of standing. The majority concluded that anthropogenic global warming was already causing rising sea waters that are taking land under the sovereignty of Massachusetts, that the rate of taking would increase over time, and that the resulting injury to Massachusetts as a sovereign was judicially cognizable even though

---

19.   549 U.S. 497 (2007).

it is "widely shared" by many others. The dissenting Justices concluded instead that any injury to Massachusetts was "pure conjecture" and, even if it was real, it was not judicially cognizable because it was a generalized injury common to "humanity at large." The dissenting Justices also concluded that any injury caused by global warming was not redressable by a court because EPA could reduce emissions of global warming gases by no more than an insignificant four per cent by taking the action it refused to take. The majority responded by noting that most attempts to challenge regulatory actions would be unsuccessful if the reasoning of the dissent was accepted because regulatory agencies routinely act in incremental ways that reduce harms on a gradual step-by-step basis.

The majority opinion in *Massachusetts* has a peculiar characteristic that makes it difficult to interpret. The majority repeatedly emphasized the importance of the interests of a sovereign state. It distinguished cases in which the petitioner was instead a private party. As the dissenting opinion argued persuasively, however, the Court had never before attached significance to state sovereignty in a standing case. It is impossible to know how important the state sovereignty issue was to the majority. The dissenting opinion argued that the standing dispute would have been resolved against the petitioners in the absence of a state among the petitioners. That is plausible. Many observers of the Court believe that Justice Kennedy was willing to join the majority opinion only because of the presence of a state as a petitioner and only because of the majority's willingness to emphasize state sovereignty as an important decisional factor.

c. Informational Injuries

The Freedom of Information Act (FOIA), discussed in chapter 12, provides a good illustration of a situation in which a party has standing to obtain review of an agency action based on an informational injury. In FOIA, Congress gave "any person" the right to obtain any information in a government record unless the information fits within one of several exemptions. Thousands of lawsuits have been brought by individuals who allege that they were denied non-exempt information they requested. Actions of that type usually produce arguments about the scope and applicability of an FOIA exemption, but they rarely, if ever, give rise to a claim that the individual who sought the information lacks standing to sue. The government and all judges and Justices appear to recognize the commonsense proposition that Congress can enact a statute that confers a right to information on one or more individuals and that any agency violation of such a statute causes a judicially cognizable informational injury to the individual who was illegally denied the information.

Yet, the invocation of informational injuries as a basis for standing has long been controversial in many contexts. Two cases that appear to be similar in most respects but that were resolved in opposite ways can help in understanding the nature and bases for the disputes that arise in this area. In its 1974 opinion in United States v. Richardson[20], the Supreme Court held that taxpayers and voters lacked standing to assert a right to require the government to disclose the budget of CIA. Article I, Section 9 of the Constitution provides that: "a regular Statement of Account of the Receipts and Expenditures of all public Money shall be published from time to time." Yet, the government refused to make public the level of expenditures by the CIA. In fact, Congress enacted a statute that prohibits anyone from disclosing the CIA budget. The Court held that the petitioners lacked standing because their injury was "abstract", "generalized" and "widely shared."

It is easy to infer the reasons for the Court's holding in Richardson, and they have nothing to do with the law of standing. The Court did not want to resolve the dispute for good reasons unrelated to standing. A literal interpretation and application of the Statement of Accounts clause would require the Court to compel the government to do something that both the Executive Branch and the Legislative Branch strongly opposed. The Court is highly unlikely to get into a fight with both of the other Branches without having a good reason for doing so. It did not have good reason in Richardson. Indeed, most if not all Justices probably agreed with Congress and the President that public revelation of the CIA's budget would harm national security. Moreover, the provision of the Constitution at issue does not appear to confer a right on anyone. The Court often uses standing as a pretext when it has other good reasons for staying out of a dispute.

A six-Justice majority distinguished Richardson in a superficially similar case in its 1998 opinion in FEC v. Akins.[21] Congress enacted a statute that requires every "political committee" to file with the FEC information with respect to the committee's sources of funds and the politicians who receive its funds. The statute also requires FEC to make available to the public all of the information filed by a political committee and gives FEC the responsibility to

20. 418 U.S. 166 (1974).   **21.** 524 U.S. 11 (1998).

determine whether an organization is a political committee. Petitioners consisted of voters who believed that an organization was a political committee and wanted to know the sources and recipients of the organization's funds. The petitioners asked FEC to determine that the organization was a political committee. When FEC found that the organization was not a political committee, the petitioners sought review and claimed to have standing attributable to an informational injury. FEC relied on *Richardson* to support its argument that the petitioners lacked standing.

The majority in *Akins* distinguished *Richardson* and held that the petitioners had standing. The majority concluded that the existence of a statute that conferred on all voters a right to information that Congress considered potentially important to their exercise of the right to vote changed the analysis and the result. The majority concluded that the statutory right to information asserted by the petitioners was not unacceptably "abstract" but was instead "sufficiently concrete and specific" to be judicially cognizable even though it was "widely shared" with all other voters. The three dissenting Justices expressed the views that *Richardson* controlled the outcome; that the petitioners lacked standing because they were asserting a "widely shared" interest; and, that Congress cannot confer standing on an individual whose interest is widely shared.

d. Procedural Injuries

The Supreme Court said nothing about the role of procedural injuries in the law of standing until its 1992 opinion in *Defenders*. That is surprising, since the vast majority of petitions to review agency actions are based on alleged procedural injuries, e.g., the agency did not provide an adequate hearing, did not provide adequate notice of a proposed rule, or did not provide an adequate explanation for its action. The plurality opinion in *Defenders* noted that an abstract procedural injury can never be sufficient to support standing. A party who alleges that is has been injured by an agency's failure to provide a required procedure must identify a concrete substantive interest that it had at stake in the proceeding in which the agency allegedly committed a procedural error that prejudiced the petitioner. The plurality also recognized, however, that when a procedural injury is coupled with a concrete substantive interest, "[t]here is much truth to the assertion that 'procedural rights' are special: The person who has been accorded a procedural right to protect his concrete interests can assert that right without meeting all of the normal standards of redressability and immediacy. Thus, ... one ... has standing to challenge ... an agency's [failure to follow a procedure] even though he cannot establish with any certainty that [provision of the procedure will change the outcome of the case]...." In other words, a petitioner can assert injury based on an agency's failure to provide a required hearing without establishing that provision of the hearing will change the outcome of the case.

C. Statutory Prerequisites of Standing

When Congress explicitly confers standing on a group that includes the petitioner, e.g., by conferring standing on "any person," the petitioner obviously fulfills the statutory prerequisites for standing, and the only question the court must answer is whether the petitioner satisfies the constitutional test for standing. Congress often does not address standing in a clear and explicit manner, however. In that common situation, a court must draw inferences based on ambiguous statutory language.

APA § 702 confers standing on "[a] person ... adversely affected or aggrieved within the meaning of a relevant statute." In its landmark opinion in *ADP*, the Supreme Court interpreted that statutory language to reflect congressional intent to confer standing on any petitioner who seeks to protect an interest that is "arguably within the zone of interests to be protected by the statute or constitutional guarantee in question." The Court has vacillated, however, with respect to its interpretation and application of the zone of interests test. The test could be interpreted to require a petitioner to prove that Congress specifically intended to protect the interests the petitioner is asserting or to allow a court to draw an inference that Congress intended to protect the interests asserted by the petitioner based on ambiguous circumstantial evidence. The choice between those two methods of interpreting and applying the test is usually determinative of the outcome of the statutory part of the standing inquiry, since Congress rarely states whether it intends to protect particular interests of potential petitioners when it enacts an agency-administered statute.

In 1987, a five-Justice majority held that competitors of banks fell within the zone of interests "arguably" to be protected by a depression-era banking regulation statute, even though the statute was intended primarily to benefit bank depositors and made no reference to the interests of competitors of banks.[22] The majority said that the zone of interests test "denies a right to review [only] if the plaintiff's interests are so marginally related to or inconsis-

---

22. Clarke v. Securities Industry Ass'n, 479 U.S. 388 (1987).

tent with the purposes implicit in the statute that it cannot be assumed that Congress intended to permit the suit." The majority explicitly stated that "there need be no indication of congressional intent to benefit the would-be plaintiff." In a 1991 opinion, however, a six-Justice majority that included the Justices who had dissented in 1987, held that a petitioner lacked standing because it had not shown that Congress intended to protect the interest it asserted in the statute that was the basis for the petitioner's claim on the merits.[23] To complete the circle, in 1998, a five-Justice majority that included the Justices who had dissented in 1991, held that a petitioner need not prove that Congress intended to protect the interests it asserted to fit within the zone of interests, and that a court should infer that Congress intended to include the petitioner's interests in the zone to be protected if a victory on the merits would further the petitioner's interests.[24] The dissenting Justices complained that the method of applying the zone of interests test adopted by the majority "eviscerates the zone of interests requirement."

As discussed in detail in § 9B, some but not all Justices believe that statutes also are relevant to resolution of the constitutional part of a standing dispute. Thus, for instance, some Justices reason that Congress can create a judicially cognizable injury in fact by enacting a statute that confers a right the violation of which then constitutes an injury,[25] and some Justices believe that courts should defer to congressional determinations that a particular remedy will redress an injury.[26] Other Justices believe that Articles II and III of the constitution limit Congress's power to convert public rights into private rights[27] and that a court should make an independent determination of whether a statutorily authorized remedy can redress an injury to private rights.[28]

---

23. Air Courier Conference of America v. American Postal Workers Union, 498 U.S. 517 (1991).

24. National Credit Union Administration v. First National Bank & Trust Co., 522 U.S. 479 (1998).

25. E.g., FEC v. Akins, 524 U.S. 11 (1998).

26. E.g., Friends of the Earth v. Laidlaw Environmental Services, 528 U.S. 167 (2000).

27. E.g., dissenting opinion in *Akins*, supra, note 25.

28. E.g., dissenting opinion in *Laidlaw*, supra, note 26.

Chapter Ten

POLITICAL CONTROLS

Administrative law courses tend to focus primarily on the relationship between courts and agencies, but the Legislative and Judicial Branches have far more control over agency actions than does the Judicial Branch. That is as it should be in a democracy in which unelected life-tenured judges are by far the least politically accountable government officials. If we do not like the way Congress or the President are shaping agency policies, we can simply vote the President or the members of Congress out of office. We would have no such recourse to the ballot box if judges and Justices exercised most of the control over agency actions. This chapter will discuss the many ways in which the politically accountable branches exercise control over agency actions and the constitutional limits on the power of the Legislative and Executive Branches to control agency actions.

A. Legislative Controls

Congress has more power over agencies than any other institution. Congress controls agency decisionmaking through its use of formal mechanisms like statutes, as well as through its use of informal mechanisms like oversight hearings, confirmation hearings, budget hearings, and jawboning by individual members.

1. Statutes

Since an agency has only the powers delegated to it by Congress, every agency action begins with enactment of a statute. Since most legally binding agency actions are subject to judicial review, most disputes that are resolved by agencies end with judicial application of one or more statutes to ensure that the agency stayed within statutory boundaries. There are thousands of statutes that authorize agencies to act. Statutes of that type are often called agency organic acts. They can be divided roughly into two categories—statutes like the Social Security, Medicare, and Medicaid Acts, that authorize agencies to implement benefit programs that account for well over fifty per cent of the U.S. budget, and statutes like the Clean Air Act, Federal Communications Act, and Occupational Safety and Health Act, that authorize agencies to implement regulatory programs that cost regulatees, and ultimately consumers, far more than the total taxes imposed by the federal government. Congress can exercise direct formal plenary control over all agency actions through the instructions it gives to agencies and reviewing courts in agency organic Acts. As discussed in Chapter two, Congress often chooses to delegate power broadly to agencies subject only to ambiguous and malleable standards, and the Supreme Court acquiesces in such congressional decisions. It is important to recognize, however, that Congress can at any time limit agency discretion to any extent it chooses by amending an agency organic act to give the agency and reviewing courts more specific instructions.

One of the reasons Congress often chooses to delegate broad power to agencies in agency organic acts is because it has access to many other statutory and non-statutory means of influencing or channeling agency actions. Many statutes in addition to agency organic acts have significant effects on agency decisionmaking. The first nine chapters of this book refer repeatedly to the most important of those statutes—the Administrative Procedure Act (APA.) By describing the procedures agencies must use to make decisions and the basic relationship between agencies and courts, the APA has major systemic effects on agency actions. Many other statutes have similar effects. They include the Freedom of Information Act and the other open government laws discussed in chapter twelve. They also include the National Environmental Policy Act (NEPA)—which requires agencies to prepare environmental impact statements whenever they consider taking a major action that will have a significant effect on the environment—the Civil Service Act—which limits the President's power to control agency actions by limiting his ability to hire, fire, promote or demote the vast majority of people who participate in agency decisionmaking—and the Information Quality Act (IQA)—which requires agencies to act only on the basis of studies and other data sources that are considered of sufficiently high quality.

Many of these statutes have subtle but powerful indirect effects that far exceed their direct formal effects. Thus, for instance, NEPA has no judicially enforceable substantive standard. Thus, in theory, an agency can prepare an impact statement that concludes that an action will have devastating effects on the environment and still take the action. Since its enactment in 1968, however, NEPA has had the effect of forcing all agencies to take environmental factors into account in their decisionmaking. Thus, it has had the effect of tilting all agency decisionmaking in more environmentally benign directions even though it is impossible to identify its effects on any particular agency action. The 1996 IQA is not even enforceable by a court.[1] Yet, it has forced agencies to pay more attention to the quality of the data they rely on in taking various actions.

Of course, none of the scores of statutes Congress has enacted in its attempts to improve agency decisionmaking has had only beneficial effects. Thus, for instance, critics of NEPA argue that it has added greatly to the cost and delay of deciding to embark on many socially-beneficial construction projects, and critics of IQA argue that it has added greatly to the cost and delay of issuing many socially-beneficial regulatory rules. All statutes have both good and bad effects. It is often difficult or impossible to determine whether a statute has net beneficial or net detrimental effects.

2. Less Formal Means of Control

In addition to the process of enacting statutes, Congress has access to many other less formal means of influencing agency actions. They include: conduct of oversight hearings that are designed to expose an agency to public criticism and, thereby, to induce it to change its approach to an issue; enactment of appropriations bills that limit or preclude an agency from using appropriated funds for specified purposes or that encourage agencies to become more active in some area by increasing the funds available for specified purposes; and refusals to confirm Presidential nominees for positions of leadership in an agency unless the nominee agrees to pursue policies that are preferred by members of Congress.

The availability of this powerful arsenal of weapons also has the effect of conferring power on individual members of Congress to influence agency actions. An individual member often can convince an agency to take an action, refrain from taking an action, or modify a planned action by threatening: to enact an amendment to an agency organic act that would restrict an agency's powers, to conduct embarrassing oversight hearings; to reduce the agency's appropriations; or, to refuse to confirm nominees to high positions in the agency. The power of an individual member varies greatly depending on such factors as membership on committees with oversight or appropriations power over an agency and the individual's persuasive power with colleagues. Of course, individual members rarely need to resort to crude tactics such as explicit threats to persuade an agency to act in a way favored by the member. Since agency heads know that at least some members of Congress have

---

1. Salt Institute v. Leavitt, 440 F.3d
156 (4th Cir. 2006).

the power to help or to hurt the agency in a wide variety of ways, agencies often change course in response to gentle and subtle urgings from particularly influential members.

3.   Constitutional Limits on Legislative Power

The Constitution imposes three important limits on the power of Congress to control agency actions. The Due Process Clause limits the circumstances in which Congress can use informal means of encouraging an agency to take a particular action in an adjudication, while the Bicameralism and Presentment Clauses preclude Congress for vetoing an action taken by an agency or from exercising control over potential removal of agency heads.

a.   Due Process

As discussed in chapter three, the Due Process Clause applies to some types of agency adjudications. In such cases, attempts by Congress to influence the outcome of the case can have the unintended effect of precluding the agency from deciding the case the way the members of Congress prefer or at least of disqualifying any potential agency decisionmaker who may have been influenced by the pressure from Congress. Thus, for instance, the D.C. Circuit disqualified all of the members of the Federal Trade Commission from having any role in deciding an antitrust case because the court concluded that Congress had conducted hearings that were so pointed in their efforts to persuade the members to decide the case in a particular manner that the defendant could not obtain a fair decision from any of the Commissioners.[2]

b.   Legislative Vetoes

During the 1970s and the early 1980s, Congress began to include in many agency organic acts, provisions that purported to grant either one House of Congress or both Houses of Congress the power to veto many actions taken by agencies. By 1983, Congress had included one House or two House legislative veto provisions in nearly two hundred agency organic acts, and Congress was considering enactment of an amendment to the APA that would have created a generic right to veto any action taken by any agency. The Supreme Court stopped the trend to add congressional vetoes to

2.   Pillsbury Co. v. FTC, 354 F.2d 952
(5th Cir. 1966).

agency-administered statutes with its 1983 opinion in INS v. Chadha,[3] in which it held that all such provisions are unconstitutional. The Court held that a two House veto violates the Presentment Clause—which requires Congress to present each Bill it votes to enact to the President, subject to potential Presidential veto, before the Bill can become law—and that the one House veto violates both the Presentment Clause and the Bicameralism Clause—which requires every Bill to be enacted by both Houses before the Bill can become law.

Congress had exercised the legislative veto powers the Court held to be unconstitutional in only a few cases. Yet, there were good reasons for concern that the existence of legislative veto provisions in agency-administered statutes was having adverse effects of two different types. First, the existence of legislative veto provisions was encouraging Congress to enact statutes that delegated broad power to agencies subject to few if any limits on agency discretion. As discussed in chapter two, legislation of that type has bad effects of various types. The existence of legislative veto provisions was encouraging Congress to enact statutes that confer broad standardless powers on agencies because influential members of Congress believed that the existence of legislative veto provisions provided them a means of persuading agencies to use their powers in ways that would please influential individual members and their constituents. Second, and closely related to the first bad effect, the existence of legislative veto provisions increased significantly the power of influential individual members of Congress to use threats to force agencies to act in the ways they preferred.

To understand these effects of legislative veto provisions, imagine one of the common situations in which an agency proposes to take an action that displeases an important constituent of an influential individual member of one House of Congress. The individual member will consider an attempt to persuade the agency to refrain from taking the action by threatening to take an action that will harm the agency. Imagine first that the agency organic act does not have a legislative veto provision. In that situation, the agency is unlikely to acquiesce in the influential member's demand unless it believes that the member can persuade a majority of members of both Houses and the President, or two-thirds of the members of both Houses, to take the action that harms the agency. That is because any legislative action that can harm the agency is subject to the requirements of Bicameralism and Presentment. Now imagine that the agency organic act contains a one House veto provision. In that situation, the agency will have no choice but to acquiesce in

---

3.   462 U.S. 919 (1983).

the influential individual member's demand if the agency believes that he can persuade a majority of his colleagues to go along with him in vetoing the agency action even if the agency believes that neither the other House of Congress nor the President would go along with the influential individual member. Thus, the legislative veto provisions were having the effect of increasing the risk of the vices of factionalism that the Framers of the Constitution were attempting to avoid by requiring Bicameralism and Presentment as prerequisites to the enactment of any statute.

In 1996, Congress enacted the Congressional Review Act (CRA). The CRA creates a version of a legislative veto, but with a big difference. Under the CRA, Congress can veto an agency action only if both Houses vote to nullify the action, Congress presents the resulting Bill to the President, and either the President acquiesces in the Bill or, if the President vetoes it, Congress overrides the veto by a two-thirds vote in each House. The version of the legislative veto authorized by the CRA is clearly constitutional because it complies with Bicameralism and Presentment. Of course, for the same reason, the CRA does not actually change the power of Congress at all. Before it enacted the CRA, Congress could do everything the CRA authorizes through a quaint process known as enactment of a statute.

c. Agencies Controlled by Congress

In its 1986 opinion in Bowsher v. Synar,[4] the Supreme Court held that Congress cannot itself control an agency that has the typical powers of an Executive Branch agency—the powers to adjudicate disputes or to issue rules. The Court generalized from its holding and reasoning in *Chadha*—Congress cannot act in any legally binding manner without complying with the requirements of Bicameralism and Presentment. It follows that Congress cannot circumvent those requirements by creating an agency that can take legally binding actions and then exercising control over that agency. The head of the agency at issue in *Bowsher* could be removed from office only through a process that began with passage of a resolution by a House of Congress. The Court concluded that the power of Congress to initiate the process of removal of the head of the agency created a situation in which the agency head was subservient to Congress.

4.   478 U.S. 714 (1986).

B. Executive Controls

1. *The Appointment Power*

The President has several ways in which he can control, or at least influence greatly, agency actions. The first, and by far the most important, is the power to appoint Officers of the United States. Article II, Section 2 provides that the President "shall nominate, and by and with the Advice and Consent of the Senate, shall appoint ... Officers of the United States ...: but the Congress may by law vest the Appointment of such inferior Officers, as they think proper, in the President alone, in the Courts of Law, or in the Heads of Departments." The Supreme Court has held that anyone who has the power to make legally binding rules, final decisions in adjudicatory disputes decided by agencies, and/or the power to prosecute or to bring an enforcement action in a court must be either an Officer or an inferior officer.[5] It has also held that an inferior Officer must be inferior in some meaningful respects to an Officer.[6] Every Officer, including every agency head, is chosen by the President. Congress occasionally vests the power to appoint an inferior Officer in a court, but the vast majority of inferior Officers are chosen either directly by the President or indirectly by the President acting through one of the department heads he previously chose. Moreover, any inferior Officer, no matter how appointed, necessarily is accountable in some important respects to an Officer chosen by the President.

The bottom line is simple. Every agency is run by people who have been chosen by the President. Since Presidents usually choose appointees who share the President's policy preferences and who have a sense of loyalty to the President, they usually exercise their powers in ways that are consistent with the President's preferences.

2. *The Removal Power*

As the Supreme Court has recognized, the power to remove a decisionmaker creates a "here and now subservience" relationship between the decisionmaker and the individual who has the power

---

5. Buckley v. Valeo, 424 U.S. 1 (1976).

6. See, e.g., Morrison v. Olson, 487 U.S. 654 (1988) (Congress can vest power to appoint an independent counsel in a court because, inter alia, independent counsel must comply with policies of Department of Justice and can be removed by the Attorney General for cause.)

to remove the decisionmaker.[7] The President has the power to remove all Officers and inferior Officers. In most cases, the President's removal power is plenary—the President can remove the Officer at any time for any reason or for no reason. In some cases, however, Congress has limited the President's removal power by statute, and the Supreme Court has upheld the statutory limit. The Court has decided five major cases involving the President's power to remove an Officer or inferior Officer.

In its 1926 decision in Myers v. United States,[8] the Supreme Court held unconstitutional a statute that limited the President's power to remove officials of the Executive Branch, in the case of Myers, a postmaster. The opinion in *Myers* contains expansive language that was initially interpreted to announce a complete prohibition on any statutory restriction on the President's power to remove any Executive Branch official. Subsequent opinions involving the removal power render such a sweeping interpretation of *Myers* impossible. Today, *Myers* must be given a much more narrow interpretation, e.g., Congress cannot restrict the President's power to remove an Officer or inferior Officer unless Congress has good reasons for doing so and the restrictions leave the President with enough authority to exercise the power conferred on him by Article II, section 3 to "take care that the laws be faithfully executed." One plausible interpretation of *Myers* today equates it with the holding in the Court's 1986 opinion in Bowsher v. Synar[9], discussed in § A(3)(c) of this chapter—Congress cannot itself exercise control over an agency by giving itself a role in the removal of an officer or inferior officer. The statute the Court held unconstitutional in *Myers* purported to prohibit the President from removing an Executive Branch official without first obtaining the consent of the Senate. Interestingly, a President's refusal to comply with that statute was the stated basis for the impeachment of President Andrew Johnson fifty years before the Court held the statute unconstitutional in *Myers*.

The Court's 1935 decision in Humphrey's Executor v. United States[10] forced observers of the Court to narrow considerably their original expansive interpretation of *Myers*. The Court upheld a statute in which Congress provided a specified term in office for an Officer, a Commissioner of the Federal Trade Commission (FTC), that exceeded the term of the President who appointed the Officer and in which Congress limited the power of the President to

7. Bowsher v. Synar, 478 U.S. 714 (1986).

8. 272 U.S. 52 (1926).

9. 478 U.S. 714 (1986).

10. 295 U.S. 602 (1935).

remove the Officer to a situation in which the President states a cause for removal. Like the opinion in *Myers*, the opinion in *Humphrey's* contained expansive language that allowed it to be interpreted as broadly as the original interpretation of *Myers*, albeit in the opposite direction, e.g, Congress can limit severely the President's removal power with respect to any Officer simply by characterizing the agency in which the Officer serves as an "independent agency."

Such a broad interpretation of *Humphrey's* is at least dubious in light of subsequent opinions. The better interpretation of *Humphrey's* today is somewhat narrower, e.g., Congress can limit the President's power to remove an Officer or inferior Officer by requiring the President to state a cause for removal if Congress can give good reasons for imposing such a limit and if the limit does not interfere with the President's ability to "take care that the laws be faithfully executed." Congress had good reasons to limit the President's power to remove an FTC Commissioner. At the time, FTC had only two functions—adjudicating disputes involving the rights of individuals and corporations and advising Congress with respect to the need to enact proposed regulatory statutes. It is at least arguable that both functions could be performed better by an agency that had some degree of independence from the power of the President. Moreover, it is impossible to determine the actual effect of a for cause limitation on the President's removal power. If the President states a cause for removing an Officer, a court might well conclude that it lacks the power to review such a Presidential decision. Even if a court concluded that a putative removal for cause presented a justiciable controversy, it might well accept as adequate cause a determination by the President that the Officer was not willing to comply with the policies of the President.[11] We cannot know the answers to these questions because no court has ever addressed them.

The Court's 1958 opinion in Wiener v. United States[12] strengthened the case for interpreting *Humphrey's* as a decision that was dependent on the functions performed by the official whose removal was at issue. Wiener was a member of the War Claims Commission, an agency that Congress created to resolve claims against the government arising out of World War II. The statute instructed the Commission to decide the claims "according to law"—a function precisely analogous to the function of a court.

---

11. See Richard Pierce, Morrison v. Olson, Separation of Powers, and the Structure of Government, 1988 Sup. Ct. Rev. 1 (1988).

12. 357 U.S. 349 (1958).

When President Eisenhower attempted to remove one of the Commissioners without stating any cause for removal, the Court held that the President could only remove a Commissioner for cause. The Court noted that Congress had assigned the Commission a task that was indistinguishable from the tasks performed by federal courts, and that federal judges are insulated from Presidential control by life-tenure, subject only to potential removal through impeachment. The Court drew the inference that Congress intended to provide some degree of insulation from Presidential control to the judge-like members of the Commission by requiring the President to state a cause for removing a Commissioner.

The Court's 1988 opinion in Morrison v. Olson provided additional support for a functional interpretation of *Humphrey's*. Morrison was an independent counsel who was appointed by a court to investigate, and potentially to prosecute, alleged wrongdoing by a senior official in the Executive Branch. The individual the independent counsel was assigned to investigate challenged the constitutionality of the statute that authorized the appointment of the independent counsel by a court of law and that insulated the independent counsel to some extent from Presidential control. The Court first held the appointment by a court of law permissible on the basis that the independent counsel was an inferior Officer. It then upheld the limitation on the President's removal power. The Court emphasized that: (1) conflict of interest concerns provided a good reason for Congress to insulate an independent counsel from presidential control to some extent, since an independent counsel's job was to investigate alleged criminal conduct by either the President or high-ranking officials in the President's Administration; (2) the independent counsel has no policymaking power; (3) the independent counsel is required to comply with the policies of the Department of Justice; and,(4) the independent counsel can be removed by the Attorney General for cause. (A few years after the Court decided *Morrison,* Congress decided that independent counsels caused more problems than they solved. Congress allowed the statute that authorized appointment of independent counsels to expire.)

It is challenging to try to extract a set of principles from the Court's first four major cases on the removal power, but here is an attempt to do so. Under no circumstances can Congress give itself any role in the removal process or insulate completely any Officer or inferior Officer from the President's power of removal. In some circumstances, Congress can limit the President's removal power by requiring him to state a cause for removal or by conferring a for cause removal power on an at will employee of the President, such as the Attorney General, instead of the President. Congress can take that action only when it can convince a court that it has a good functional reason for doing so, e.g., to provide some degree of insulation from Presidential control for judge-like agency decision-makers or for people who are charged with responsibility to investigate and/or prosecute the President and/or high ranking members of his Administration. It is not at all clear that Congress can limit the President's power to remove an Executive Branch official who has any policymaking power.

In any event, it is unlikely that the limits on the President's power to remove agency officials have significant effects. In over 200 years, only two government officials—Myers and Wiener—tried to block a Presidential removal decision, and only one—Wiener—succeeded. (Humphrey died shortly after he was removed, and his estate brought an action for back pay.) Government officials who were appointed by the President almost invariably "resign" if the President asks for their resignations because they are almost always individuals who are loyal to the President and to his political party. The few government officials who were appointed by a prior President and who serve a term of years that allows them to remain in office after the election of a new President rarely stay for more than a few months. The only agency officials who are in that category are members of multi-member Commissions, like the Federal Trade Commission. They know that: (1) the new President will be able to name a new Chair of the Commission immediately; (2) because of predictable resignations, the new President will have appointed a majority of the Commissioners within seven months; (3) if their policy preferences differ from those of the appointees of the new President, their role will be limited to writing dissenting opinions within a few months; and, (4) they can almost always get a much better paying job elsewhere after adding the title "former Commissioner" to their resume.

Many administrative law scholars and many members of Congress have attached great significance to the Supreme Court's opinion in *Humphrey's* and have used statutory limits on the President's removal power as a basis for characterizing some agencies as "independent" of the Executive Branch, rather than part of the Executive Branch. There are passages in the opinion in *Humphrey's* that support that interpretation, e.g.: "the FTC was not to be subject to anybody in the government but ... only to the people of the United States." To the extent that interpretation of *Humphrey's* was supportable when the opinion was first issued, it has become totally insupportable in light of many subsequent opinions and of contemporary understandings of the permissible structure of government. The Constitution recognizes only three Branches of government; Congress cannot create a third. The FTC cannot be directly accountable to the people because the Commissioners are not elected. The FTC must be accountable to Congress to a considerable extent, since Congress has the power to enact or amend statutes that change or eliminate its powers, the power to refuse to confirm nominees to be members of the Commission, and the power to determine whether and to what extent to appropriate funds to allow it to operate. The FTC must be accountable to the President because the President has the power to nominate Commissioners, to designate the Chair, and to remove Commissioners, albeit subject to the requirement that the President state a cause for removal.

To the extent that there is anything to the characterization of an agency as "independent," its independence has little if anything to do with the modest, rarely invoked statutory requirement that the President state a cause for removing a Commissioner. Agencies that are characterized as "independent" typically have several statutory characteristics in common, in addition to fixed, staggered terms in office for Commissioners and a requirement that the President state a cause for removing a Commissioner. They are headed by a collegial body consisting of three, five, or seven Commissioners, no more than a bare majority of whom can be members of the same political party. (The D.C. Circuit has held that the constitutionality of the statutory political party restriction on the composition of independent agencies is not a justiciable question.)[13] As a practical matter, it is much more difficult for the President to exercise the kind of informal influence over an agency that is described in section 3 when the agency is headed by a multi-member body some of whom are members of the opposition party than it is for the President to exercise that kind of informal influence over an agency headed by a single individual who is a member of the President's party. Moreover, Presidents have been reluctant to subject independent agencies to the kinds of systematic controls that are discussed in section 4 because of fear that Congress would become upset and would be less willing to work with the President in other areas of policymaking.

It is important to remember that all agencies, including pure Executive branch agencies, are to a considerable extent "independent" of the President if, and to the extent that, they resolve adjudicatory disputes that are subject to the Due Process Clause. See § 3D. All such adjudications must be resolved by a "neutral decisionmaker," who must be insulated to a considerable extent

13. FEC v. NRA Political Victory Fund, 6 F.3d 821 (D.C. Cir. 1993).

from all outside influences, including efforts by the President to influence the outcome of such an adjudication.

In Free Enterprise Fund v. Public Accounting Oversight Board[14], the Supreme Court held that Congress cannot limit the President's constitutional power to "take care that the laws be faithfully executed" by providing *two* (or more) layers of for-cause insulation of an officer or inferior officer from presidential control. In other words, Congress cannot provide that an inferior officer can only be removed for cause by an officer who can only be removed by the President for cause. In a dissenting opinion, Justice Breyer listed thousands of inferior officers whose insulation from potential removal by the President would seem to be in jeopardy after the Court's decision.

3. *Informal Influence*

Any President can have enormous influence over any agency policy decision, including any rulemaking. He need only pick up the phone and call his appointee or summon him to the White House to communicate his strong policy preferences. In the vast majority of circumstances, the appointee acts in accordance with the preferences expressed by the President. The D.C. Circuit has explicitly approved this practice,[15] and the Supreme Court has implicitly approved it.[16] In the rare case in which an appointee refuses to act in accordance with the President's preferences, the President must decide whether to remove the official (or ask for his resignation) or whether to yield to the preferences of the appointee. That is a political decision that depends on the significance the President attaches to the policy issue at stake versus the value the President attaches to retaining the services of the appointee.

Every President undoubtedly has used this form of ad hoc intervention in agency decisionmaking to influence many decisions. It is impossible to provide more specific data or analysis of this common practice, however, because it is almost always done quietly and privately. Investigative journalists discover and report on only a tiny fraction of cases of this type.

14. ___ U.S. ___, 130 S.Ct. 3138 (2010).

15. Sierra Club v. Costle, 657 F.2d 298 (D.C. Cir. 1981), discussed in § 4B(2)(a).

16. Chevron v. NRDC, 467 U.S. 837 (1984), discussed in chapter five.

1. Systematic controls

Every President from Franklin Roosevelt to the present has complained of an inability to control the sprawling bureaucracy. So many agencies take so many actions that implement or reflect federal policy that the President cannot possibly be aware of most of the actions, much less attempt to coordinate policy among agencies or to insure that agencies are implementing the policies preferred by the President (and presumptively, a majority of the electorate). Every modern President has taken actions that are intended to increase Presidential ability to influence and to coordinate agency policymaking.

The most important single action was the issuance of Executive Order 12,291 by President Reagan. That order applies to any major rulemaking engaged in by an Executive Branch agency, with "major" defined to include any rule that was expected to require incurrence of at least one hundred million dollars per year in regulatory costs. E.O. 12,291 requires an agency to calculate the costs and benefits of each proposed rule and alternatives to the proposed rule and to choose the alternative that will produce the largest estimated net benefits. As with all such Executive Orders, it recognizes implicitly that an agency may not be able to comply with one or more of its provisions because of inconsistent instructions in an applicable statute. It requires agencies to comply only to the extent that compliance is consistent with statutes. Thus, for instance, if an agency rule is being issued pursuant to a statute that prohibits the agency from considering costs in issuing rules, E.O. 12, 291 still requires the agency to calculate the costs and benefits of the proposed rule, but the agency is not required to consider costs in deciding whether to issue the rule.

E.O. 12,291 also requires agencies to submit major rules they intend to issue to the Office of Information and Regulatory Analysis (OIRA) in the White House Office of Management and Budget (OMB). It authorizes OIRA to require the agency to delay issuance of the rule until OIRA has had an adequate opportunity to review it. E.O. 12,291 also authorizes OIRA to require the agency to meet with OIRA or with other agencies with interests in the rulemaking to consider making changes in the proposed rule that are suggested by OIRA or by another interested agency and/or to consider data or analysis that OIRA or another interested agency consider important to the agency's decisionmaking.

President Reagan also issued Executive Order 12,498. That Order recognizes implicitly the major limitation on the efficacy of E.O. 12,291—it authorizes White House involvement in the rulemaking/policymaking process so late in the decisionmaking process that the President can have little practical effect. By the time a major proposed rule is subjected to the OIRA review process, the agency typically has devoted years of study and tens of thousands of staff hours to the decisionmaking process. At that point, OIRA can realistically expect to have only modest incremental effects on the final version of the rule. E.O. 12,498 was intended to allow the White House to exercise more effective control by allowing OIRA to become involved in the decisionmaking process that leads to issuance of a major rule at a much earlier stage. E.O. 12,498 required agencies to issue periodic regulatory agendas in which they describe each major rulemaking they are undertaking or have under consideration and the expected timetable for acting with respect to each major rulemaking.

E.O. 12,498 was intended to allow OIRA to become involved in agency rulemakings at an early stage. It has had limited effects of that type, however, because OIRA lacks the staffing required to play that role. E.O. 12,498 has had another effect, however, that has indirectly increased the ability of the President to coordinate and influence agency policymaking. The regulatory agendas issued by agencies assist the political appointees who occupy the highest positions in the agency in their often challenging efforts to find out what their agency is doing or planning to do. That information, in turn, helps the political appointees become involved more effectively in the decisionmaking process that eventually produces a major rule.

President Bush (41) left E.O. 12,291 and 12,498 intact. President Clinton replaced both with E.O. 12,866. The Clinton Executive Order incorporated all of the basic elements of the Reagan Order, but it also made important changes. It added time limits and transparency rules to the OIRA review process. Those changes responded to the criticisms of the OIRA review process, as implemented by Presidents Reagan and Bush (41), as unduly long and so opaque that outsiders had no way of knowing what was happening in the process.

President Bush (43) retained the Clinton Order with one change. Presidents Reagan, Bush (41), and Clinton had designated the Vice President as the person who was authorized to resolve any disputes between agencies and OIRA that arise during the review process. President Bush (43) deleted that provision from the Order, reflecting Vice President Cheney's apparent desire not to play any official role in the OIRA review process. Vice President Cheney has played major roles in the informal process of influencing agency actions, however. In an investigative report aptly titled "Leaving No Tracks," the Washington Post reported many cases in which

Vice President Cheney engaged in highly effective informal control of agency actions.[17] Thus, for instance, when a severe drought forced the Department of Interior (DOI) to choose between allowing crops to die and allowing salmon to die, and DOI initially made the decision to operate its dams in such a way as to preserve the salmon and sacrifice the crops, Vice President Cheney called a low level political appointee at DOI and directed her to reverse the decision. She complied immediately. This anecdote illustrates an important point. Any President can, and does, exercise powerful influence over agency decisionmaking through both publicly visible systematic processes like OIRA review of major rules and through largely invisible ad hoc informal exercises in jawboning political appointees.

Recent Presidents have engaged in other means of influencing the agency decisionmaking process in addition to the OIRA review process. Of course, the differing nature of those measures reflects the differing degrees of enthusiasm for federal regulation of each President. Thus, for instance, President Clinton often took personal "ownership" of a rulemaking by directing an agency to initiate a rulemaking to issue a rule governing some high visibility health or safety problem.[18] Conversely, President Bush (43) took three actions that were designed to reduce excessive or unduly burdensome regulation. He directed OIRA to enforce vigorously the Information Quality Act that Congress enacted in 1996 to preclude agencies from relying on low quality data sources as the basis for regulatory actions and he instructed OIRA to implement a procedure through which regulatees could nominate unduly burdensome rules as candidates for rescission.

The Justice Department has repeatedly concluded that the President can extend the rulemaking review procedure to "independent agencies," but no President has been willing to take that action to date for fear of alienating Congress.[19]

---

17. Jo Becker & Barton Gellman, Leaving No Tracks, The Washington Post A1 (June 27, 2007).

18. See Elena Kagan, Presidential Administration, 114 Harv. L. Rev. 2245 (2001).

19. For discussion of this issue and many others that surround the review process, see the Symposium on the Occasion of the Thirtieth Anniversary of OIRA, 63 Admin. L. Rev. 1 (2011).

Chapter Eleven

AGENCY POWER TO INVESTIGATE

A. Introductory Overview

Agencies typically have extraordinarily broad statutory powers to investigate, including broad powers to require reports, to issue subpoenas, and to inspect premises. Exercise of those powers is limited by the Fourth Amendment prohibition on unreasonable searches and seizures and the Fifth Amendment privilege against self-incrimination. Until the 1940s, the Supreme Court interpreted statutes that gave agencies investigative powers narrowly and interpreted the Fourth and Fifth Amendment restrictions on agency investigative powers broadly. Beginning in the 1940s, however, and continuing through the present, courts have interpreted agency statutory grants of investigative powers broadly and have interpreted the Fourth and Fifth Amendment restrictions on the exercise of those powers narrowly. As a result, agencies can exercise extremely broad investigative powers today; most regulated firms comply "voluntarily" with agency reporting requirements and subpoenas; and, firms rarely challenge agency exercises of investigative powers in court. When they do, they usually lose. The following two sections summarize the evolution of this area of law and its present state in the contexts of agency exercises of the power to require reports and the subpoena power and the power to inspect premises and records.

B. Mandatory Reports and the Subpoena Power

Until the 1940s, the Supreme Court interpreted statutory grants of power to require reports and subpoena power to agencies narrowly and interpreted Fourth and Fifth Amendment restrictions on the exercise of those powers broadly. Thus, for instance, in opinions issued in 1924 and 1936, the Court held that an agency could only obtain judicial enforcement of a subpoena by demonstrating that it had probable cause to believe that the subject of the subpoena had committed a violation of law that was within the agency's jurisdiction and that the information sought was relevant to that violation.[1] The Court labeled any broader scope attempt to exercise an agency's subpoena power as a "fishing expedition"

1. Jones v. SEC, 298 U.S. 1 (1936); 298 (1924).
FTC v. American Tobacco Co., 264 U.S.

which was a violation of the Fourth Amendment and "contrary to the first principles of justice." The Court also interpreted the Fifth Amendment to prohibit compulsory production of books and records.

In a 1943 opinion, however, the Supreme Court upheld an agency subpoena and rejected a lower court's effort to determine whether the information sought was needed to investigate alleged wrongdoing in the agency's jurisdiction.[2] The Court said that the question of whether the information sought was relevant to a violation of law in the agency's jurisdiction was for the agency, rather than the court, to determine. The Court held that a court must enforce an agency subpoena if the evidence sought is "not plainly incompetent or irrelevant to any lawful purpose of the" agency.

The Court reaffirmed and broadened that holding in a 1946 opinion in which it also changed completely its interpretation of the Fifth Amendment in the context of agency subpoenas for records.[3] It held that the Fifth Amendment provided no protection against compulsory production of corporate records unless the subpoena is unreasonable in its scope or lacking in specificity. The Court later extended that holding to partnerships[4] and even to individuals.[5]

Finally, in 1950, the Court confronted and retracted its oft-stated condemnation of "fishing expeditions," with the recognition that: "Even if one were to regard the request for information in this case as caused by nothing but official curiosity, ... agencies have a legitimate right to satisfy themselves that corporate behavior is consistent with the law...."[6] Today, a regulated firm has virtually no chance of success in convincing a court not to enforce an agency rule that requires reports from regulatees or an agency subpoena unless the firm can establish that the material sought is unreasonably broad and burdensome to provide or that the subpoena violates some clear statutory restriction of the agency's power. Victories for regulatees on either of those theories are rare.

C. Agency Inspections

In companion cases decided in 1967, the Supreme Court held that an agency inspection of premises is unreasonable and violates

2. Endicott Johnson Corp. v. Perkins, 317 U.S. 501 (1943).

3. Oklahoma Press Publishing Co. v. Walling, 327 U.S. 186 (1946).

4. Bellis v. United States, 417 U.S. 85 (1974).

5. Andresen v. Maryland, 427 U.S. 463 (1976).

6. United States v. Morton Salt Co., 338 U.S. 632 (1950).

the Fourth Amendment unless the agency has a warrant.[7] The Court also held, however, that a court can issue a warrant authorizing a search by a regulatory agency without a showing of probable cause to believe that the owner of the premises is violating the law. Instead, a judge or magistrate can issue a warrant to an agency authorizing the agency to inspect a large number of premises if the agency can show that it has a regulatory justification for conducting the inspections. It is so easy for an agency to satisfy the standard for a warrant that most regulatees routinely consent to warrantless inspections rather than risk angering the agency by putting it to the trouble of obtaining a warrant. An agency needs neither a warrant nor consent to inspect premises if the business at issue has traditionally been subject to regulation. Inspection of premises involved in production or sale of liquor[8] or firearms[9] and health and safety inspection of mines[10] fall within this category, but health and safety inspection of manufacturing premises does not.[11]

---

7. See v. Seattle, 387 U.S. 541 (1967); Camara v. San Francisco, 387 U.S. 523 (1967).

8. Colonnade Catering Corp. v. United States, 397 U.S. 72 (1970).

9. United States v. Biswell, 406 U.S. 311 (1972).

10. Donovan v. Dewey, 452 U.S. 594 (1981).

11. Marshall v. Barlow's, 436 U.S. 307 (1978).

Chapter Twelve

FREEDOM OF INFORMATION ACT AND OTHER OPEN GOVERNMENT ACTS

Congress has enacted several statutes that are designed to make the agency decisionmaking process more transparent and accessible to the public. The four most important are discussed in this chapter—the Freedom of Information Act (FOIA), the Privacy Act (PA), the Government in the Sunshine Act (GSA), and the Federal Advisory Committee Act (FACA).

A. The Freedom of Information Act

FOIA confers on "any person" a right to obtain information contained in any "agency record" unless the information falls within one of ten exemptions.

1. Disclosure to Any Person

FOIA confers on "any person" a right to obtain information contained in any "agency record" unless the information falls within one of ten exemptions. FOIA is used by investigative reporters, interested members of the public, lawyers, regulatees, organized crime syndicates, and foreign intelligence agencies. Congress and courts are well aware that FOIA can be used for such laudatory purposes as exposure of government corruption or incompetence and for such odious purposes as identification of government informants and sources of U.S. intelligence for assassination by crime syndicates or foreign intelligence agents. That awareness forces Congress to draft, and courts to interpret and apply, the exemptions from the duty to disclose with sensitivity to the potential high costs of inappropriate disclosure as well as the benefits of disclosure. An "agency record" is defined broadly to include any record, paper or electronic, that has been created or retained by an agency and that is in the control of the agency.[1]

---

1. Department of Justice v. Tax Analysts, 492 U.S. 136 (1989); Forsham v. Harris, 445 U.S. 169 (1980); Kissinger v. Reporters Committee for Freedom of Press, 445 U.S. 136 (1980).

2. *Timing and Cost of Disclosure*

Shortly after FOIA went into effect in 1967, Congress began to receive widespread complaints that agencies were delaying interminably their responses to FOIA requests. Congress responded by amending FOIA to require an agency to respond to each request with either the information requested or a statement of reasons why the information is exempt from disclosure within twenty days of the receipt of a request. Agencies rarely comply with that statutory deadline. In fact, agencies sometimes require twenty years, rather than twenty days, to respond to a FOIA request.[2] The principal source of this problem is the unwillingness of Congress to appropriate funds sufficient to allow agencies to comply with FOIA requests in a timely manner. Congress initially estimated that the total cost of compliance with FOIA would be $100,000 per year. The actual cost of compliance is approximately 100,000 times greater than that estimate, but Congress has never been willing to provide adequate funding to allow agencies to comply in a timely manner.

The combination of the high cost of compliance and the congressional unwillingness to provide funding has produced great frustration among individuals who make FOIA requests and among the courts that must interpret and apply FOIA. In its 1976 opinion in Open America v. Watergate Special Prosecution Force,[3] the D.C. Circuit responded to this problem with an unusual decision. It refused to enforce the twenty-day statutory deadline. It concluded that, given the inadequate funding of FOIA compliance, judicial enforcement of the deadline at the behest of a requester who sues would require agencies to place the requests of those who sue in the cue ahead of the requests of those who do not. The court concluded that Congress did not intend to require agencies to favor requests by those who sue over requests of those who do not, so it refused to enforce the statutory deadline. Every other circuit has since agreed with the D.C. Circuit, but courts regularly address FOIA delay cases because agencies often delay to the point at which a court is willing to intervene. Since the root of the problem of delay is inadequate funding, however, courts can do little but criticize an agency's delay.

Congress responded to the related problems of high compliance costs, inadequate funding, and systemic delay with two amendments to FOIA. First, in 1986, Congress amended FOIA by autho-

---

2. See Fiduccia v. Department of Justice, 185 F.3d 1035 (9th Cir. 1999).   **3.** 547 F.2d 605 (D.C. Cir. 1976).

rizing OMB to issue Guidelines that agencies could use to charge fees to some categories of requesters. Requesters are placed in one of four categories—"commercial use requesters," "education and non-commercial scientific institution requesters," "requesters who are representatives of the news media," and "all other requesters." The first group is charged the "full direct costs of searching for, reviewing for release, and duplicating the records sought," a total cost that can exceed a million dollars.[4] The second and third groups are charged the cost of reproduction only, minus the cost of reproducing the first 100 pages. The fourth group is charged the same as the first group, minus the cost of the first two hours of search time and the cost of reproducing the first one hundred pages. An agency is required to waive all fees, however, if "disclosure of the information is in the public interest"—interpreted by courts to include information that the requester will make readily available to the public and that contributes significantly to public understanding of government operations.[5] Second, in 1996, Congress amended FOIA by requiring agencies to give expedited treatment to requests where the request demonstrates a compelling need for the information—interpreted by courts to refer to information concerning matters of "current exigency to the American public"[6]—and by authorizing agencies to give expedited treatment to other requests determined by the agency.

3. Exemptions

There are ten exemptions from the duty to disclose. An agency can exercise its discretion to make available information that is exempt from the duty to disclose unless the requested information is protected from disclosure by another statute or by an agency rule. If a request is made for exempt information that is protected from disclosure by another statute or by an agency rule, an individual or firm that would be injured by provision of the information can obtain an injunction prohibiting its provision by filing an action pursuant to APA § 706 alleging that provision of the information is not "in accordance with law."[7]

4. E.g., OSHA Data v. Department of Labor, 220 F.3d 153 (3d Cir. 2000) (upholding $1.7 million fee).

5. Judicial Watch v. Rossotti, 326 F.3d 1309 (D.C. Cir. 2003).

6. Al–Fayed v. CIA, 254 F.3d 300 (D.C. Cir. 2001).

7. Chrysler Corp. v. Brown, 441 U.S. 281 (1979).

a. Exemption One: National Security

The first exemption applies to matters that are "specifically required by Executive Order to be kept secret in the interest of national defense or foreign policy." The President can, and has, delegated the power to make classification decisions that exempt information to departments and agencies. Courts are authorized to engage in in camera review to determine whether a classification decision was appropriate, but courts are extremely reluctant to second-guess agency classification decisions,[8] and an agency can avoid in camera review by providing the court a detailed affidavit explaining why the information sought is exempt.[9]

b. Exemption Two: Internal Personnel Rules

The second exemption applies to internal agency personnel rules and practices. Until 2011, many circuit courts had interpreted it to apply to any rule that applied primarily to internal matters. In 2011, however, the Court held that it applied only to personnel rules.[10]

c. Exemption Three: Information Exempted by Other Statutes

The third exemption applies to information that is "specifically exempted from disclosure by statute" but only if the statute gives the agency no discretion to disclose or gives the agency discretion to disclose only when specified criteria are satisfied. The third exemption requires regular judicial interpretation and application in the contexts of scores of other statutes that exempt information from disclosure in myriad circumstances.

d. Exemption Four: Trade Secrets

The fourth exemption covers "trade secrets and commercial or financial information obtained from a person and privileged or confidential." Hundreds of cases interpret "trade secret" for state law purposes, but the D.C. Circuit has held that the definition is narrower for FOIA purposes.[11] The "privileged or confidential" information component of the fourth exemption has produced a lot of litigation and differences of opinion among circuit courts. The

---

8. Halperin v. CIA, 629 F.2d 144 (D.C. Cir. 1980).

9. Military Audit Project v. Casey, 656 F.2d 724 (D.C. Cir. 1981).

10. Milner v. Navy, ___ U.S. ___, 131 S.Ct. 1259 (2011).

11. Public Citizen Health Research Group v. FDA, 704 F.2d 1280 (D.C. Cir. 1983).

D.C. Circuit applies the exemption to (1) information that is provid
ed voluntarily to an agency if it is of a type that is not customarily
disclosed to the public and to (2) information that is provided
pursuant to a mandatory duty to provide the information if disclosure would impair the government's ability to obtain information in
the future or cause substantial harm to the competitive interests of
the individual or firm that provided the information.[12] By contrast,
the Second Circuit presumes that information provided pursuant to
a mandatory agency requirement is not exempt and that a firm has
waived its claim of confidentiality if it provides the information
voluntarily to an agency in litigation.[13]

e. Exemption Five: Inter–Agency and Intra–Agency Memoranda

The fifth exemption applies to "inter-agency or intra-agency
memorandums or letters that would not be available by law to a
private party in litigation with the agency." The fifth exemption
incorporates the rules governing discovery and evidentiary privileges, except that the work product privilege is absolute, rather
than qualified, in the context of the exemption.[14] Pre-decisional
documents that reflect the reasoning or deliberations of an agency
or its personnel are privileged and exempt because their disclosure
would discourage "frank discussion of legal and policy issues," but
factual materials contained in such documents are not exempt.[15]
Final decisions of agencies, including any reasoning the agency
relies on to support its decision, are not exempt because they are
"effective law and policy."[16] The fifth exemption also incorporates
Executive Privilege, the constitutionally-based privilege of the President to refuse to disclose confidential communications he receives
from advisors. The D.C. Circuit has extended the scope of that
privilege to cover communications that the President never receives
if they were requested by a Presidential advisor to assist the
President in making a decision that is exclusively in his power,[17]
and the Supreme Court has relied on the Constitution to create a
related privilege applicable to confidential communications from

12. Critical Mass Energy Project v. NRC, 975 F.2d 871 (D.C. Cir. en banc 1992).

13. Inner City Press v. Federal Reserve System, 463 F.3d 239 (2d Cir. 2006); In re Steinhardt Partners, 9 F.3d 230 (2d Cir. 1993).

14. FTC v. Grolier, 462 U.S. 19 (1983).

15. EPA v. Mink, 410 U.S. 73 (1973).

16. NLRB v. Sears, Roebuck & Co., 421 U.S. 132 (1975).

17. In re Sealed Case, 121 F.3d 729 (D.C. Cir. 1997).

advisors to the Vice President.[18]

f. Exemption Six: Personal Privacy

The sixth exemption applies to personal information "the disclosure of which would constitute a clearly unwarranted invasion of privacy." The Supreme Court interprets the sixth exemption to require a balancing of the public interest in disclosure and the individual's interest in privacy.[19] It interprets the interest in personal privacy broadly to include any information about an individual the disclosure of which might cause harm to the person and the public interest in disclosure narrowly to apply only to information the disclosure of which would contribute significantly to public understanding of government activities.[20]

g. Exemption Seven: Law Enforcement Records

The seventh exemption applies to "records or information compiled for law enforcement purposes, but only to the extent that the production of such ... records or information...." After that language there follows two pages of provisions that begin with either "would" or "could reasonably be expected to," e.g., "could reasonably be expected to interfere with law enforcement proceedings." This long and complicated exemption has an unfortunate history. The original version of the exemption was short and simply applied to all law enforcement records. When members of the public complained that it was too broad, Congress amended it in 1974 to apply only when production of a law enforcement record would cause one of six specific forms of harm. A few years later, Congress discovered that the narrower version of the exemption was causing serious damage of many types, e.g., it was being used to identify police informants and undercover officers for assassination and it was being used to identify enforcement methodologies so that criminals could commit crimes in ways that involved less likelihood of detection. Congress responded by amending the exemption again in 1986 to create the version that exists today. The 1986 amendments consisted of the addition of many other forms of harm that could cause information to fall within the exemption and a significant reduction in the agency's burden to prove that disclosure

18. Cheney v. United States District Court for the District of Columbia, 542 U.S. 367 (2004).

19. Department of State v. Ray, 502 U.S. 164 (1991).

20. Department of Defense v. FLRA, 510 U.S. 487 (1994).

would cause one of the identified forms of harm by substituting "could reasonably be expected to" for "would" in many subsections. The net effect of the 1986 amendments is to make it difficult to convince an agency or court to disclose any law enforcement record or any information contained in such a record, with law enforcement defined broadly to include civil, administrative, and criminal investigations.

h. Exemption Eight: Records of Financial Institutions

The eighth exemption is extremely broad. It covers all information contained in records or reports of any agency responsible for regulating financial institutions.

i. Exemption Nine: Oil Well Data

The ninth exemption is narrow. It applies to "geological or geophysical information and data, including maps containing wells." It is redundant, since anything that falls within its scope also would qualify as a trade secret or confidential information within the scope of the fourth exemption.

j. Exemption Ten: Critical Infrastructure

In the wake of the September 11, 2001 terrorist attack on the United States, Congress created a new exemption from FOIA applicable to information concerning critical infrastructure. Congress was in such a hurry to do something to reduce the risk of terrorism that it actually enacted two versions of the critical infrastructure exemption, with two different definitions of critical infrastructure. Both definitions are extremely broad, but only time will tell how agencies and courts will interpret and apply the critical infrastructure exemption.

B. The Privacy Act

The Privacy Act requires agencies to maintain only accurate records about individuals, provides an individual a right to obtain any information about him or her contained in an agency's records, provides a mechanism for requiring an agency to correct errors in an individual's records, limits strictly the circumstances in which an agency can make public personal information about an individual, and provides a cause of action for damages for any individual who is damaged by a violation of the Act.

C. Sunshine Act

The Government in the Sunshine Act (GSA) applies to any agency that is headed by a multi-member body, e.g., FTC, FCC, and FERC. It requires such agencies to announce all meetings of the Commissioners and meeting agendas in advance, make meetings open to the public, and transcribe meetings. It has exemptions that are generally analogous to the exemptions to FOIA with a notable exception. GSA has no exemption analogous to FOIA exemption five—the exemption applicable to inter-agency and intra-agency memoranda. That omission was intentional. Its inclusion would have been inconsistent with the basic belief that underlay congressional enactment of GSA—government and the public are best served when all deliberations leading to a decision are conducted in public. Of course, the entirety of GSA is inconsistent with the basic belief that underlay the congressional decision to include exemption five in FOIA—high quality decision-making depends on robust and candid debate which can only take place in private.

GSA has terrible effects, including: Commissioners rarely meet, meetings are typified by stilted and scripted remarks instead of candid and robust debate, and most decisions are made outside of meetings through a process of notational voting in which each Commissioner merely notes his or her agreement or disagreement with a proposed decision. Fortunately, the Supreme Court was able to avoid another bad effect of GSA by interpreting it not to apply to U.S. participation in international conferences designed to facilitate joint and coordinated policymaking.[21] No other country was willing to participate in such meetings with the U.S. if GSA required all meetings of the international conferences to be conducted in public.

D. Advisory Committee Act

The Federal Advisory Committee Act (FACA) was enacted to ensure that any outside group that advises the government is balanced in the interests and viewpoints it represents and that any advice it gives is formulated and transmitted in a transparent manner. FACA has several provisions that are designed to ensure that agencies create balanced advisory committees. The transparency goal is furthered by requiring that all advisory committees meet in public and by requiring such committees to make all documents they consider or compile accessible to the public. The public meeting requirement is subject to exemptions analogous to the exemptions in GSA, while the document disclosure requirement is subject to exemptions analogous to the exemptions in FOIA.

21. FCC v. ITT World Communications, 466 U.S. 463 (1984).

Congress clearly intended that FACA apply to committees that advise the President, but courts have not so interpreted it, for good reason. In 1989, a five-Justice majority of the Supreme Court held that FACA does not apply to the ABA Committee that advises the President with respect to potential judicial nominees.[22] The majority applied the avoidance canon and stretched the language of FACA to avoid having to hold it unconstitutional as a violation of separation of powers. The dissenting Justices interpreted FACA to apply to the committee and would have held FACA unconstitutional in its application to groups that advise the President.

The D.C. Circuit has followed the Supreme Court's lead and has relied on the avoidance canon to stretch the language of FACA when FACA otherwise might violate the Constitution. Thus, for instance, when it was called upon to decide whether the Health Care Task Force that Hillary Clinton headed was an advisory committee that routinely met in private in violation of FACA, the court held that the Task Force was not an Advisory Committee because it consisted only of government employees, including forty "temporary" government employees whose status was tenuous at best, and the President's wife, who would seem not to fit comfortably in the category of government employee.[23] Similarly, when it was called upon to decide whether the unidentified group of individuals who advised Vice President Cheney with respect to the national energy policy he announced was an illegal advisory committee, the court held that it was not an advisory committee because no private individual had a formal right to vote on any matter under consideration.[24]

22. Public Citizen v. Department of Justice, 491 U.S. 440 (1989).

23. Association of American Physicians and Surgeons v. Clinton, 997 F.2d 898 (D.C. Cir. 1993).

24. In re Cheney, 406 F.3d 723 (D.C. Cir. en banc 2005).

Chapter Thirteen

PRIVATE RIGHTS OF ACTION FOR VIOLATIONS OF AGENCY ADMINISTERED STATUTES

Agency resources available to enforce agency-administered statutes are always scarce. An agency-administered statute can have more powerful effects on behavior if it can also be enforced directly by beneficiaries who are injured by violations of the statute or of rules adopted to implement the statute. Deciding whether to authorize private rights of action to enforce an agency-administered statute raises difficult public policy questions, however, because private rights of action also can have serious adverse effects. There are two well-known disadvantages of a private right of action for violation of an agency-administered statute. First, authorizing courts to enforce provisions of agency-administered statutes can create inconsistency and/or incoherence with respect to the meaning of the statute. Indeed, conflicting interpretations are virtually inevitable any time that more than one institution has the authority and responsibility to interpret the same statute. Second, private enforcement can have more complicated and subtle adverse effects in forms such as interference with the agency's enforcement strategy or over-deterrence of conduct that arguably constitutes a technical violation of a statute but that actually has net beneficial effects on society and on pursuit of the policies of the President. Congress frequently enacts statutes that are inconsistent in their policy implications and effects. The Supreme Court has recognized that only the President or institutions within his control have the practical ability to act in ways that make sense of conflicting statutes. Thus, for instance, in a 2007 opinion the Supreme Court concluded that two agency-administered statutes conflicted with each other and deferred to the agency's method of attempting to reconcile the conflict.[1]

A private right of action to enforce an agency-administered statute can have one of three sources—explicit creation of a private right of action by Congress in the statute at issue, judicial implica-

---

1. National Ass'n of Home Builders   (2007).
v. Defenders of Wildlife, 551 U.S. 644

tion of a private right of action, or judicial interpretation of the statute to create a federal statutory right that is enforceable against states, localities, and their employees in a civil rights action filed pursuant to 42 U.S.C. § 1983, a provision of the Civil Rights Act of 1871. Each of these potential sources is discussed in a section of this chapter.

A.   Express Private Rights of Action

Congress sometimes includes in an agency-administered statute a provision that explicitly authorizes a private right of action for damages, injunctive relief, and/or civil penalties for violation of an agency-administered statute and/or agency rules issued to implement a statute. Thus, for instance, Congress has included provisions in fourteen environmental regulation statutes that authorize "any citizen" to sue an individual or firm that violates the statute and to obtain an injunction prohibiting future violations and/or civil penalties for past violations of the statute, plus attorney's fees. Express private rights of action provisions raise two types of issues. First, complaints filed pursuant to such provisions often give rise to serious disputes with respect to the standing of the individual plaintiff to bring the action, as discussed in chapter nine. Second, they frequently require courts to interpret the statute and/or agency rules at issue.

One recurring question is whether Congress has authorized a private right of action only for violation of the statute, only for violation of rules or orders issued to implement the statute, or for both. Once a court resolves that initial interpretative dispute, it often must resolve a second set of questions—whether Congress authorized private rights of action for violations of all provisions of the statute and/or all rules and orders issued pursuant to the statute and, if not, which provisions, rules, and/or orders fall within the scope of the private right of action. Once a court has resolved this second set of interpretative disputes, it often must resolve a third set of issues—has the plaintiff complied with all of the statutory prerequisites for filing a private right of action? Finally, the court must grapple with a fourth set of issues—what is the meaning of the statutory provision, rule, or order that was arguably violated, and did the individual or firm actually violate that provision, rule, or order? A pair of cases decided by the Supreme Court in 1989 and 2007 illustrate some of the typical interpretive questions that arise in express private right of action cases.

In its 1989 opinion in Hallstrom v. Tillamook County,[2] the Supreme Court interpreted and applied the express private right of

---

2.   493 U.S. 20 (1989).

action provision in the Resource Conservation and Recovery Act (RCRA). Like many private right of action provisions, the private right of action provision in RCRA was carefully crafted to minimize conflicts between EPA, the agency charged with implementing RCRA, and courts that receive complaints filed pursuant to the private right of action provision. Thus, for instance, private rights of action are authorized only for violations of rules issued to implement RCRA, rather than for violations of RCRA itself, in order to minimize potential conflicts between EPA's understanding of RCRA and the understanding of courts that entertain private rights of action based on RCRA. The RCRA private right of action provision also has prerequisites for filing a private right of action that are designed to minimize potential conflicts between EPA's enforcement strategies and private actions. A private party can sue to enforce a RCRA rule against an alleged violator only after it has given the violator and the state and federal agencies responsible for enforcing RCRA 60–days notice of its intent to file a private right of action. In *Hallstrom*, the Court held that courts must interpret and apply that prerequisite to the filing of a private right of action strictly to further the congressional "goal of giving environmental agencies, rather than courts, the primary responsibility for enforcing RCRA."

In 2007, the Justices divided in the process of interpreting and applying the private right of action provision in the Communications Act in Global Crossing Telecommunications v. Metrophones Telecommunications.[3] In a sense, that provision is the opposite of the provision in RCRA. It authorizes a private right of action only for violation of a provision of the Communications Act and not for violation of an agency rule that implements the Act. Congress sometimes makes that choice because it wants to authorize private enforcement only of its own rules, in the form of statutory provisions, and not of agency rules issued to implement the statute. A seven-Justice majority held that the district court could enforce the private right of action provision in a case in which one provider of communications services alleged that another service provider had damaged it by violating the Communications Act, as the Act had been interpreted by FCC. Two Justices dissented based on their conclusion that the conduct at issue did not constitute a violation of the statute, but only a violation of a rule issued to implement the statute.

3.   550 U.S. 45 (2007).

B. Implied Private Rights of Action

In its 1964 opinion in J.I. Case v. Borak,[4] the Supreme Court held that section 14(a) of the Securities & Exchange Act can be enforced through private actions for damages filed by individuals who have been damaged by conduct that violates that provision. The statute did not authorize private rights of action, but the Court implied such a right of action based on its belief that, since Congress wanted the provision to be effective, it must have wanted courts to authorize private parties to supplement the agency's scarce enforcement resources.

The Court's reasoning in *Borak* was simplistic and naïve. The Court failed to recognize that the decision to incorporate a private right of action in an agency-administered statute requires some institution to make a complicated and difficult policy decision in which it balances the benefits and costs of private rights of action. Indeed, even if an institution makes the decision to incorporate a private right of action in an agency-administered statute, it must make a long series of related policy decisions with respect to the scope of the private right of action and the prerequisites to bringing such an action.

Since the *Borak* Court failed to recognize the nature and difficulty of the decision to include a private right of action in an agency-administered statute, it failed to engage in careful evaluation of the characteristics of the alternative institutions that might make such a decision. Once the Court recognized that the decision whether to incorporate a private right of action in an agency-administered statute requires some institution to make a series of difficult public policy decisions, it concluded that Congress, rather than a court, should make all such decisions. It took the Court almost forty years of gradual changes to the *Borak* holding before it reached that conclusion and reflected it in a clear holding, however.

The Court backed away considerably from the simplistic reasoning in *Borak* in its 1975 decision in Cort v. Ash.[5] The Court announced a new four-part test to determine whether a court should imply a private right of action in an agency-administered statute. One of the parts of the test was whether there is "any indication of legislative intent, explicit or implicit, either to create such a remedy or to deny one." In later cases, the Court emphasized the importance of the legislative intent part of the *Cort* test and emphasized its reluctance to accept anything except explicit

4. 377 U.S. 426 (1964).   5. 422 U.S. 66 (1975).

statutory language as sufficient evidence of legislative intent to create a private right of action.[6]

The Court finally broke completely with its reasoning and holding in *Borak* in its 2001 opinion in Alexander v. Sandoval.[7] Technically, the only holding in *Alexander* is limited to a determination of the scope of a private right of action that the Court had previously held to be implied in a statute. In its opinion, however, the Court criticized harshly its prior opinions in cases like *Borak* and *Cort,* in which it had implied private rights of action in statutes that did not explicitly authorize private rights of action. The Court then described its present quite different approach:

> [P]rivate rights of action ... must be created by Congress....
> Statutory intent on this ... point is determinative.... Without
> it a cause of action does not exist and courts may not create
> one, no matter how desirable that might be as a policy mat-
> ter,....

After *Alexander*, it is nearly impossible to convince a court to conclude that an agency-administered statute authorizes a private right of action unless the statute explicitly creates such a right. The Court had already implied quite a few private rights of action before it decided *Alexander*, however.

C. Rights Enforceable Through § 1983

The third potential source of a private right of action is a judicial decision holding that a provision of an agency-administered statute is enforceable in a suit filed pursuant to 42 U.S.C. § 1983, although such a right of action can be enforced only against a state or local government or an individual acting under color of state law. Section 1983 is part of the Civil Rights Act of 1871. It was originally enacted for the important, but narrow, purpose of providing a means through which newly-freed slaves could protect their constitutional rights from the Ku Klux Klan. In the late 1970s and 1980s, however, the Supreme Court broadened § 1983 in many ways. As interpreted in those cases, it authorized a citizen to obtain damages from an individual acting under color of state law, a state, or a local government that intentionally deprives the individual of a federal constitutional or statutory right, including rights conferred in agency-administered statutes,[8] and potentially rights created by

---

6. E.g., Suter v. Artist M., 503 U.S. 347 (1992).

7. 532 U.S. 275 (2001).

8. Maine v. Thiboutot, 448 U.S. 1 (1980) (§ 1983 applies to federal statuto-ry rights as well as constitutional rights); Monell v. Department of Social Services of the City of New York, 436 U.S. 658 (1978) (§ 1983 applies to local governments); Carey v. Piphus, 435 U.S. 247 (1978) (public employees are poten-

federal agency rules.[9]

By 2002, it was apparent that a plaintiff who could no longer persuade a court to imply a private right of action in an agency-administered statute because of the Court's 2001 decision in *Alexander*, discussed in the prior section, could obtain the same result by persuading a court that the agency-administered statute created a right that could be enforced through an action brought pursuant to § 1983. In its 2002 opinion in Gonzaga University v. Doe,[10] the Court attempted to reconcile the conflict between its decisions refusing to imply private rights of action in agency-administered statutes and its decisions interpreting § 1983 to create a private right of action to enforce many provisions of agency-administered statutes. The Court rejected "the notion that our implied right of action cases are separate and distinct from our § 1983 cases." It continued: "A court's role in discerning whether personal rights exist in the § 1983 context ... should not differ from its role in discerning whether private right exist in the implied private right of action context.... Both inquiries simply require a determination as to whether Congress intended to confer individual rights on a class of beneficiaries...." It follows that an agency rule can never create a right enforceable under § 1983 because only Congress can create such a right and that a typical agency-administered statute that imposes a duty and instructs an agency to enforce the duty can never create a right enforceable under § 1983 because only a statute that explicitly confers a right on identifiable individuals can create such a right.

tially liable for compensatory and punitive damages).

9. Wright v. Roanoke Redevelopment & Housing Authority, 479 U.S. 418 (1987).

10. 536 U.S. 273 (2002).

Chapter Fourteen

TORT ACTIONS AGAINST AGENCIES AND AGENCY OFFICIALS

The APA authorizes a court to reverse and remand an agency action when it concludes that the agency action is unlawful in some respect. The APA does not authorize a court to require an agency or an agency employee to pay damages to an individual or a firm that has been harmed by an unlawful action taken by the agency or agency employee, however. From time-to-time, some legislators, judges, and Justices have concluded that making damage actions available against agencies and agency employees that cause damage through unlawful actions would provide desirable additional incentives to encourage agencies and their employees to remain within the boundaries of law. This chapter discusses each of the three major means through which Congress and the courts have attempted to use tort remedies to encourage agencies and their employees to refrain from engaging in unlawful conduct that harms individuals and firms—the Federal Tort Claims Act (FTCA), the doctrine announced by the Supreme Court in Bivens v. Six Unknown Named Agents of the Federal Bureau of Narcotics,[1] and 42 U.S.C. § 1983.

A. Federal Tort Claims Act

The APA does not waive sovereign immunity in the context of damage claims against the government. Congress has enacted about forty statutes in which it has waived sovereign immunity in the context of damage claims. Most of those statutes apply only in narrow circumstances, but FTCA authorizes claims for money damages against the United States broadly whenever negligent or other wrongful acts or omissions that would constitute a tort under state law if the conduct at issue was engaged in by a private party causes damage to an individual or firm. The government is vicariously liable for the tortuous conduct of an employee if the employee was acting within the scope of his or her duties. A party who claims to have been damaged by conduct that falls in the scope of FTCA must submit a claim for compensation to the agency that was allegedly responsible for the damage and allow that agency six

---

1. 403 U.S. 388 (1971).

months in which to pay or deny the claim before the party can file an FTCA action.

FTCA has numerous exemptions, including claims by military personnel and claims that fall in several categories of intentional torts. From an administrative law perspective, the most important exemption applies to discretionary functions. That exemption insulates a high proportion of arguably erroneous agency actions from potential government liability. FTCA exempts the government from liability for:

> Any claim ... based upon the exercise or performance or failure to exercise or perform a discretionary function or duty on the part of a federal agency or an employee of the Government, whether or not the discretion involved be abused.[2]

In a pair of cases decided in the 1950s, the Supreme Court seemed to draw a distinction between decisions made at the planning level and decisions made at the operational level. Thus, it held that the government was not liable for a disastrous explosion that killed hundreds of people because any arguably negligent decisions were made at the planning level,[3] but it held that the government was liable for damages attributable to a shipwreck because the negligence consisted of a failure to inspect a lighted aid to navigation—negligence at the operational level.[4] In a 1963 opinion, the Court distinguished between exercises of policymaking discretion that are exempt and exercises of other forms of discretion, such as medical discretion, that are not exempt.[5] In a 1984 opinion, the Court recognized the importance of agency rules to application of the discretionary function exemption—if an agency exercises discretion that it confers on itself through issuance of a rule, its conduct and that of its employees is exempt from liability even if the discretion is arguably abused.[6]

The Supreme Court laid the foundation for modern interpretations of the discretionary function exemption in its 1988 opinion in Berkowitz v. United States[7] and its 1991 opinion in United States v. Gaubert.[8] In Berkowitz, the Court held that the government was liable for harm caused by negligent failure to inspect a batch of vaccine or negligent approval of a batch of vaccine after the agency

---

2. 28 U.S.C. § 2680(a).

3. Dalehite v. United States, 346 U.S. 15 (1953).

4. Indian Towing Co. v. United States, 350 U.S. 61 (1955).

5. United States v. Muniz, 374 U.S. 150 (1963).

6. United States v. S.A. Empresa de Viacao Aerea Rio Grandense, 467 U.S. 797 (1984).

7. 486 U.S. 531 (1988).

8. 499 U.S. 315 (1991).

determined that the batch failed to comply with a statute because a statute imposed on an agency a mandatory duty to inspect every batch of vaccine and a mandatory duty not to approve a vaccine if it failed to meet statutory standards. In *Gaubert,* the Court held that the government was not liable for over $100 million in damages caused by the arguably negligent conduct of a regulatory agency and its employees because no statute or rule required the agency or its employees to take particular non-discretionary actions in the circumstances presented.

The *Berkowitz/Gaubert* opinions rejected the planning versus operational distinction the Court had announced in the 1950s. After *Berkowitz* and *Gaubert*, the government is exempt from liability even for otherwise negligent acts that are "routine and frequent" if they involve the exercise of policy-based discretion. The *Berkowitz/Gaubert* Court announced a new test for applying the discretionary function test. The government is liable if a statute or rule requires an agency or its employees to act in a particular way, and the agency or its employees act in a manner inconsistent with the non-discretionary duties imposed by the statute or rule. By contrast, the conduct of an agency or its employees is exempt if the applicable statute and rules confer some degree of discretion on the agency and its employees, and the arguably negligent conduct at issue involves the exercise of policy-based discretion.

It is difficult to prevail in an FTCA action based on the conduct of an agency or its employees under the *Berkowitz/Gaubert* test because statutes rarely impose mandatory, non-discretionary duties on agencies, and agencies rarely impose such duties on themselves or their employees by rule. Most statutes and rules impose only broad duties that are susceptible to policy-based exercises of discretion, and even abuses of discretion and arguably negligent exercises of discretion are insulated from FTCA liability by the discretionary function exception.

Circuit courts sometimes disagree with respect to the application of the *Berkowitz/Gaubert* test. Most of the differences are based on the difficulty of distinguishing between exempt policy-based exercises of discretion and non-exempt exercises of other types of discretion. Thus, for instance, the Third Circuit once held that no exercises of science-based discretion fell within the scope of the exemption, but it overruled that precedent in 2001 in an opinion in which it held that at least some, and perhaps even all, exercises of science-based discretion also qualify as exempt exercises of policy-based discretion because most if not all science-based exercises of discretion require an agency to balance conflicting values.[9]

Circuit courts frequently differ with respect to the question whether agency decisions and behavior that are motivated by lack of adequate resources qualify as exercises of policy-based discretion. The question arises with great frequency because a high proportion of the damage caused by the conduct of agencies and their employees is attributable to lack of adequate resources, e.g., failures to inspect, low quality inspections, failures to warn of hazards, and decisions to use materials and techniques that create avoidable health and safety risks. Many of the conflicting circuit court opinions are cited and discussed in the opinions of a divided panel of the Tenth Circuit in 1995.[10] Courts are in a no win situation in resolving this class of cases. The root of the problem is the unwillingness of Congress to appropriate sufficient funds to allow agencies to fulfill their statutory responsibilities in an adequate manner. Thus, allowing agencies to escape liability when their actions and inactions attributable to inadequate resources cause harm tends to gut FTCA, while imposing liability in such circumstances merely aggravates the problem by taking resources from agencies that already lack adequate resources.[11]

B. *Bivens* Actions

In its 1971 opinion in Bivens v. Six Unknown Named Agents of the Federal Bureau of Narcotics,[12] the Supreme Court held that individual government employees can be held liable for damages caused by their violations of the Fourth Amendment prohibition on unreasonable searches and seizures. In opinions issued in 1979 and 1980, the Court held that the *Bivens* remedy applies to all violations of constitutional rights.[13] Thus, it would seem that individuals damaged by agency decisions that deprived them of social security disability benefits without using procedures that complied with Due Process would have a *Bivens* remedy against the government employees who made the decisions. Yet, the Court held in 1988 that the individuals could not maintain a *Bivens* action because they had access to alternative statutorily-provided remedies for the violations committed by the employees.[14]

9. Orthopedic Bone Screw Product Liability Litigation, 264 F.3d 344 (3d Cir. 2001).

10. Domme v. United States, 61 F.3d 787 (10th Cir. 1995).

11. See Richard Pierce, Judicial Review of Agency Actions in a Period of Diminishing Agency Resources, 49 Admin. L. Rev. 61 (1997).

12. 403 U.S. 388 (1971).

13. Carlson v. Green, 446 U.S. 14 (1980); Davis v. Passman, 442 U.S. 228 (1979).

14. Schweiker v. Chilicky, 487 U.S. 412 (1988).

The Supreme Court's opinion refusing to allow a *Bivens* action by Social Security beneficiaries who were damaged by unconstitutional actions taken by government employees is one of three opinions in which the Court has refused to make a *Bivens* remedy available to an individual on the basis that the individual had access to an alternative remedy.[15] That line of cases renders a *Bivens* remedy unavailable against agency employees that cause damage through conduct that violates the Constitution in a high proportion of cases. The Court has also refused to apply *Bivens* liability to agencies,[16] to government contractors that perform functions that previously were performed exclusively by government agencies,[17] and even to individual government employees that engage in unconstitutional conduct that the Court fears may be difficult to distinguish from aggressive conduct that is not unconstitutional.[18] Given the many cases in which the Court has qualified the scope of the *Bivens* remedy and/or refused to extend it to new contexts, it is hard to avoid drawing the inference that a majority of the Justices now believe that *Bivens* was a mistake that should be confined narrowly.

If an individual who is harmed by unconstitutional actions taken by an agency employee is successful in persuading a court to make a *Bivens* remedy potentially available, the individual must then overcome the employee's inevitable defense that his or her action fell within the scope of a privilege. Any action taken by a judge, prosecutor, or legislator, or by an agency employee whose functions are analogous to those of a judge, a prosecutor, or a legislator are protected by an absolute privilege.[19] The actions of other agency employees are subject to qualified immunity.[20] Qualified immunity shields an employee from immunity unless he or she violates a "clearly established" right which "a reasonable person would have known."[21]

C. Section 1983 Actions

As discussed in § 13C, 42 U.S.C. § 1983 confers a damage action on individuals harmed by agency actions in some circum-

15. See also Chappell v. Wallace, 462 U.S. 296 (1983); Bush v. Lucas, 462 U.S. 367 (1983).

16. FDIC v. Meyer, 510 U.S. 471 (1994).

17. Correctional Services Corp. v. Malesko, 534 U.S. 61 (2001).

18. Wilkie v. Robbins, 551 U.S. 537 (2007).

19. Lake Country Estates v. Tahoe Regional Planning Agency, 440 U.S. 391 (1979); Butz v. Economou, 438 U.S. 478 (1978).

20. Malley v. Briggs, 475 U.S. 335 (1986).

21. Harlow v. Fitzgerald, 457 U.S. 800 (1982).

stances. An individual who is injured by a violation of the Constitution or of an individual right created by a federal statute by someone who is acting under color of law has a cause of action for damages against the government employee who committed the violation and/or against the state or local government that took the action. As in the case of *Bivens* actions, however, the plaintiff must overcome defenses based on absolute or qualified privilege.

TABLE OF CASES

References are to Pages.

173

Office of Personnel Management v.
Richmond, 496 U.S. 414, 110 S.Ct.
2465, 110 L.Ed.2d 387 (1990), 49
Ohio Valley Water Co. v. Borough of Ben
Avon, 253 U.S. 287, 40 S.Ct. 527, 64
L.Ed. 908 (1920), 111
Oklahoma Press Pub. Co. v. Walling,
327 U.S. 186, 66 S.Ct. 494, 90 L.Ed.
614 (1946), 150
Open America v. Watergate Special
Prosecution Force, 547 F.2d 605, 178
U.S.App.D.C. 308 (D.C.Cir.1976), 94,
153
Orthopedic Bone Screw Product Liabili-
ty Litigation, In re, 264 F.3d 344 (3rd
Cir.2001), 170
OSHA Data/CIH, Inc. v. United States
Dept. of Labor, 220 F.3d 153 (3rd
Cir.2000), 154

Pacific Gas & Elec. Co. v. Federal Power
Commission, 506 F.2d 33, 164
U.S.App.D.C. 371 (D.C.Cir.1974), 78
Pacific States Box & Basket Co. v.
White, 296 U.S. 176, 56 S.Ct. 159, 80
L.Ed. 138 (1935), 42
Panama Refining Co. v. Ryan, 293 U.S.
388, 55 S.Ct. 241, 79 L.Ed. 446
(1935), 8
Paul v. Davis, 424 U.S. 693, 96 S.Ct.
1155, 47 L.Ed.2d 405 (1976), 31
Pax Co. of Utah v. United States, 454
F.2d 93 (10th Cir.1972), 104
PBGC v. LTV Corp., 496 U.S. 633, 110
S.Ct. 2668, 110 L.Ed.2d 579 (1990),
18, 19, 26, 45
Perry v. Sindermann, 408 U.S. 593, 92
S.Ct. 2694, 33 L.Ed.2d 570 (1972), 29
Personal Watercraft Industry Ass'n v.
Department of Commerce, 48 F.3d
540, 310 U.S.App.D.C. 364 (D.C.Cir.
1995), 67
Pillsbury Co. v. F.T.C., 354 F.2d 952
(5th Cir.1966), 136
Portland Cement Ass'n v. Ruckelshaus,
486 F.2d 375, 158 U.S.App.D.C. 308
(D.C.Cir.1973), 66
Professionals and Patients for Custom-
ized Care v. Shalala, 56 F.3d 592 (5th
Cir.1995), 78
Public Citizen v. United States Dept. of
Justice, 491 U.S. 440, 109 S.Ct. 2558,
105 L.Ed.2d 377 (1989), 160
Public Citizen Health Research Group v.
FDA, 704 F.2d 1280, 227 U.S.App.
D.C. 151 (D.C.Cir.1983), 155
PUC v. United States, 355 U.S. 534, 78
S.Ct. 446, 2 L.Ed.2d 470 (1958), 112
Purisch v. Tennessee Technological Uni-
versity, 76 F.3d 1414 (6th Cir.1996),
32

Reno v. Catholic Social Services, Inc.,
509 U.S. 43, 113 S.Ct. 2485, 125
L.Ed.2d 38 (1993), 109
Richardson v. Perales, 402 U.S. 389, 91
S.Ct. 1420, 28 L.Ed.2d 842 (1971), 41
Richardson, United States v., 418 U.S.
166, 94 S.Ct. 2940, 41 L.Ed.2d 678
(1974), 119, 129
Riverkeeper, Inc. v. Collins, 359 F.3d
156 (2nd Cir.2004), 101

S.A. Empresa de Viacao Aerea Rio Gran-
dense (Varig Airlines), United States
v., 467 U.S. 797, 104 S.Ct. 2755, 81
L.Ed.2d 660 (1984), 168
Salt Institute v. Leavitt, 440 F.3d 156
(4th Cir.2006), 135
Schlesinger v. Reservists Committee to
Stop the War, 418 U.S. 208, 94 S.Ct.
2925, 41 L.Ed.2d 706 (1974), 119
Schweiker v. Chilicky, 487 U.S. 412, 108
S.Ct. 2460, 101 L.Ed.2d 370 (1988),
170
Seacoast Anti–Pollution League v. Cos-
tle, 572 F.2d 872 (1st Cir.1978), 24
Sealed Case, In re, 121 F.3d 729, 326
U.S.App.D.C. 276 (D.C.Cir.1997), 156
SEC v. Chenery Corp., 332 U.S. 194, 67
S.Ct. 1575, 91 L.Ed. 1995 (1947), 57,
72
See v. City of Seattle, 387 U.S. 541, 87
S.Ct. 1737, 18 L.Ed.2d 943 (1967),
151
Shalala v. Guernsey Memorial Hosp.,
514 U.S. 87, 115 S.Ct. 1232, 131
L.Ed.2d 106 (1995), 73
Shaughnessy, United States ex rel. Ac-
cardi v., 347 U.S. 260, 74 S.Ct. 499,
98 L.Ed. 681 (1954), 18
Shinseki v. Sanders, 556 U.S. 396, 129
S.Ct. 1696, 173 L.Ed.2d 532 (2009),
40
Sierra Club v. Costle, 657 F.2d 298, 211
U.S.App.D.C. 336 (D.C.Cir.1981), 63,
145
Sierra Club v. Morton, 405 U.S. 727, 92
S.Ct. 1361, 31 L.Ed.2d 636 (1972),
122
Sims v. Apfel, 530 U.S. 103, 120 S.Ct.
2080, 147 L.Ed.2d 80 (2000), 115
Skidmore v. Swift & Co., 323 U.S. 134,
65 S.Ct. 161, 89 L.Ed. 124 (1944), 88
Skinner v. Mid–America Pipeline Co.,
490 U.S. 212, 109 S.Ct. 1726, 104
L.Ed.2d 250 (1989), 9
Steel Co. v. Citizens for a Better Envi-
ronment, 523 U.S. 83, 118 S.Ct.
1003, 140 L.Ed.2d 210 (1998), 121,
125
Steinhardt Partners, L.P., In re, 9 F.3d
230 (2nd Cir.1993), 156

INDEX

References are to Pages

182	*INDEX*
References are to Pages

†